Lab Manual

Module A

HOLT McDOUGAL

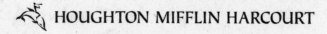

HOUGHTON MIFFLIN HARCOURT

Acknowledgements for Covers

Front cover: *DNA molecule* (bg) ©Carl Goodman/Meese Photo Research; *false color X-rays on hand* (l) ©Lester Lefkowitz/Getty Images; *primate* (cl) ©Bruno Morandi/The Image Bank/Getty Images; *red cells* (cr) ©Todd Davidson/Getty Images; *fossils* (r) ©Yoshihi Tanaka/amana images/Getty Images

Printed in the U.S.A.

ISBN 978-0-547-59254-1

5 6 7 8 9 10   0982   20 19 18 17 16 15 14 13 12
4500364970   A B C D E F G

Contents

Unit 2 Reproduction and Heredity

Using Your *ScienceFusion* Lab Program

Your *ScienceFusion* Lab Program is designed to include activities that address a variety of student levels, inquiry levels, time availability, and materials. In this Lab Manual, you will find that each student activity is preceded by Teacher Resources with valuable information about the activity.

Activity Type: Quick Lab

Each lesson within each unit is supported by two to three short activities called Quick Labs. Quick Labs involve simple materials and set-up. The student portion of each Quick Lab should take less than 30 minutes. Each Quick Lab includes Teacher Resources and one Student Datasheet.

Activity Types: Exploration Lab, Field Lab, and S.T.E.M. Lab

Each unit is supported by one to four additional labs that require one or more class periods to complete. Each Exploration, Field, and S.T.E.M. Lab includes Teacher Resources and two Student Datasheets. Each Student Datasheet is targeted to address different inquiry levels. Below is a description of each lab:

- **Exploration Labs** are traditional lab activities. The labs are designed to be conducted with standard laboratory equipment and materials.
- **Field Labs** are lab activities that are partially or completely performed outside the classroom or laboratory.
- **S.T.E.M. Labs** are lab activities that focus on Science, Technology, Engineering, and Math skills.

Inquiry Level

The inquiry level of each activity indicates the level at which students direct the activity. An activity that is entirely student-directed is often called Open Inquiry or Independent Inquiry. True Open or Independent Inquiry is based on a question posed by students, uses experimental processes designed by students, and requires students to find the connections between data and content. These types of activities result from student interest in the world around them. The *ScienceFusion* Lab Program provides activities that allow for a wide variety of student involvement.

- DIRECTED **Inquiry** is the least student-directed of the inquiry levels. Directed Inquiry activities provide students with an introduction to content, a procedure to follow, and direction on how to organize and analyze data.

- GUIDED **Inquiry** indicates that an activity is moderately student-directed. Guided Inquiry activities require students to select materials, procedural steps, data analysis techniques, or other aspects of the activity.

- INDEPENDENT **Inquiry** indicates that an activity is highly student-directed. Though students are provided with ideas, partial procedures, or suggestions, they are responsible for selecting many aspects of the activity.

Each Quick Lab includes one Student Datasheet that is written to support the inquiry level indicated on the Teacher Resources. Each Exploration Lab, Field Lab, and S.T.E.M. Lab includes two Student Datasheets, each written to support an inquiry level. In addition, the Teacher Resources includes one or more modification suggestions to adjust the inquiry level.

Student Level

The *ScienceFusion* Lab Program is designed to provide successful experiences for all levels of students.

- BASIC activities focus on introductory content and concepts taught in the lesson. These activities can be used with any level of student, including those who may have learning or language difficulties, but they may not provide a challenge for advanced students.

- GENERAL activities are appropriate for most students.

- ADVANCED activities require good understanding of the content and concepts in the lesson or ask students to manipulate content to arrive at the learning objective. Advanced activities may provide a challenge to advanced students, but they may be difficult for average or basic-level students.

Lab Ratings

Each activity is rated on three criteria to provide you with information that you may find useful when determining if an activity is appropriate for your resources.

- **Teacher Prep** rating indicates the amount of preparation you will need to provide before students can perform the activity.

- **Student Setup** rating indicates the amount of preparation students will need to perform before they begin to collect data.

- **Cleanup** rating indicates the amount of effort required to dispose of materials and disassemble the set-up of the activity.

Teacher Notes

Information and background that may be helpful to you can be found in the Teacher Notes section of the Teacher Resources. The information includes hints and a list of skills that students will practice during the activity.

Science Kit

Hands-on materials needed to complete all the labs in the Lab Manual for each module have been conveniently configured into consumable and non-consumable kits. Common materials provided by parents or your school/district are not included in the kits. Laboratory equipment commonly found in most schools has been separately packaged in a Grades 6–8 Inquiry Equipment Kit. This economical option allows schools to buy equipment only if they need it and can be shared among teachers and across grade levels. For more information on the material kits or to order, contact your local Holt McDougal sales representative or call customer service at 800-462-6595.

Online Lab Resources

The *ScienceFusion* Lab Program offers many additional resources online through our web site thinkcentral.com. These resources include:

Teacher Notes, Transparencies, and **Copymasters** are found in the Online Toolkit. Student-friendly tutorial Transparencies are available to print as transparencies or handouts. Each set of Transparencies is supported by Teacher Notes that include background information, teaching tips, and techniques. Teacher Notes, Transparencies, and Copymatsters are available to teach a broad range of skills.

- **Modeling Experimental Design** Teacher Notes and Transparencies cover Scientific Methods skills, such as Making Qualitative Observations, Developing a Hypothesis, and Making Valid Inferences.

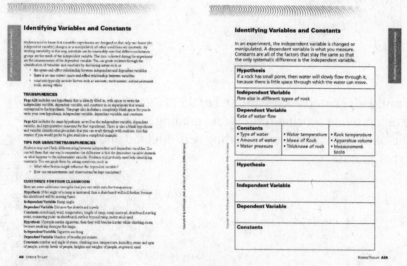

- **Writing in the Sciences** Teacher Notes and Transparencies teach written communication skills, such as Writing a Lab Report and Maintaining a Science Notebook. In addition, the Lab Report Template provides a structured format that students can use as the basis for their own lab reports.

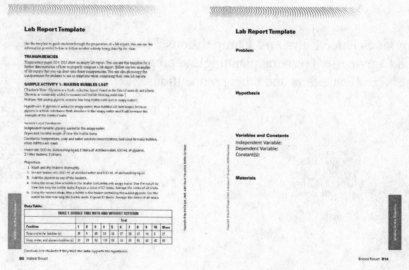

- **Math in Science Tools** Teacher Notes and Transparencies teach the math skills that are needed for data analysis in labs. These Teacher Notes and Transparencies support the S.T.E.M. concepts found throughout the *ScienceFusion* program.

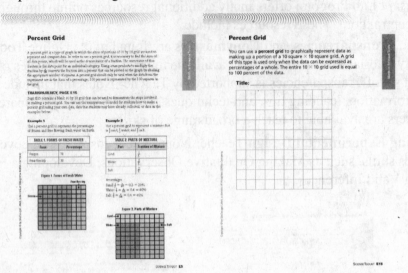

- **Rubrics and Integrated Assessment** Teacher Notes and Copymasters provide scoring rubrics and grading support for a range of student activities including self-directed and guided experiments.

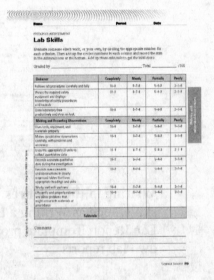

- **Planning for Science Fairs and Competitions** Teacher Notes and Copymasters provide planning and preparation techniques for science fairs and other competitions.

Making Your Laboratory a Safe Place

Concern for safety must begin before any activity in the classroom and before students enter the lab. A careful review of the facilities should be a basic part of preparation for each school term. You should investigate the physical environment, identify any safety risks, and inspect your work areas for compliance with safety regulations.

The review of the lab should be thorough, and all safety issues must be addressed immediately. Keep a file of your review, and add to the list each year. This will allow you to continue to raise the standard of safety in your lab and classroom.

Many classroom experiments, demonstrations, and other activities are classics that have been used for years. This familiarity may lead to a comfort that can obscure inherent safety concerns. Review all experiments, demonstrations, and activities for safety concerns before presenting them to the class. Identify and eliminate potential safety hazards.

1. **Identify the Risks** Before introducing any activity, demonstration, or experiment to the class, analyze it and consider what could possibly go wrong. Carefully review the list of materials to make sure they are safe. Inspect the equipment in your lab or classroom to make sure it is in good working order. Read the procedures to make sure they are safe. Record any hazards or concerns you identify.

2. **Evaluate the Risks** Minimize the risks you identified in the last step without sacrificing learning. Remember that no activity you perform in the lab or classroom is worth risking injury. Thus, extremely hazardous activities, or those that violate your school's policies, must be eliminated. For activities that present smaller risks, analyze each risk carefully to determine its likelihood. If the pedagogical value of the activity does not outweigh the risks, the activity must be eliminated.

3. **Select Controls to Address Risks** Even low-risk activities require controls to eliminate or minimize the risks. Make sure that in devising controls you do not substitute an equally or more hazardous alternative. Some control methods include the following:

   • Explicit verbal and written warnings may be added or posted.

   • Equipment may be rebuilt or relocated, parts may be replaced, or equipment be replaced entirely by safer alternatives.

   • Risky procedures may be eliminated.

   • Activities may be changed from student activities to teacher demonstrations.

4. **Implement and Review Selected Controls** Controls do not help if they are forgotten or not enforced. The implementation and review of controls should be as systematic and thorough as the initial analysis of safety concerns in the lab and laboratory activities.

Safety with Chemicals

Label student reagent containers with the substance's name and hazard class(es) (flammable, reactive, etc.). Dispose of hazardous waste chemicals according to federal, state, and local regulations. Refer to the MSDS for recommended disposal procedures. Remove all sources of flames, sparks, and heat from the laboratory when any flammable material is being used.

Material Safety Data Sheets

The purpose of a Material Safety Data Sheet (MSDS) is to provide readily accessible information on chemical substances commonly used in the science laboratory or in industry. The MSDS should be kept on file and referred to BEFORE handling ANY chemical. The MSDS can also be used to instruct students on chemical hazards, to evaluate spill and disposal procedures, and to warn of incompatibility with other chemicals or mixtures.

Storing Chemicals

Never store chemicals alphabetically, as this greatly increases the risk of promoting a violent reaction.

Storage Suggestions

1. Always lock the storeroom and all its cabinets when not in use.
2. Students should not be allowed in the storeroom and preparation area.
3. Avoid storing chemicals on the floor of the storeroom.
4. Do not store chemicals above eye level or on the top shelf in the storeroom.
5. Be sure shelf assemblies are firmly secured to the walls.
6. Provide anti-roll lips on all shelves.
7. Shelving should be constructed out of wood. Metal cabinets and shelves are easily corroded.
8. Avoid metal, adjustable shelf supports and clips. They can corrode, causing shelves to collapse.
9. Acids, flammables, poisons, and oxidizers should each be stored in their own locking storage cabinet.

Safety with Animals

It is recommended that teachers follow the NABT Position Statement "The Use of Animals in Biology Education" issued by the National Association of Biology Teachers (available at www.nabt.org).

Safety In Handling Preserved Materials

The following practices are recommended when handling preserved specimens:

1. NEVER dissect road-kills or nonpreserved slaughterhouse materials.
2. Wear protective gloves and splash-proof safety goggles at all times when handling preserving fluids and preserved specimens and during dissection.
3. Wear lab aprons. Use of an old shirt or smock under the lab apron is recommended.
4. Conduct dissection activities in a well-ventilated area.
5. Do not allow preservation or body-cavity fluids to contact skin. Fixatives do not distinguish between living or dead tissues. Biological supply firms may use formalin-based fixatives of varying concentrations to initially fix zoological and botanical specimens. Some provide specimens that are freezedried and rehydrated in a 10% isopropyl alcohol solution. Many suppliers provide fixed botanical materials in 50% glycerin.

Reduction Of Free Formaldehyde

Currently, federal regulations mandate a permissible exposure level of 0.75 ppm for formaldehyde. Contact your supplier for Material Data Safety Sheet (MSDS) that details the amount of formaldehyde present as well as gas-emitting characteristics for individual specimens. Prewash specimens (in a loosely covered container) in running tap water for 1–4 hours to dilute the fixative. Formaldehyde may also be chemically bound (thereby reducing danger) by immersing washed specimens in a 0.5–1.0% potassium bisulfate solution overnight or by placing them in 1% phenoxyethanol holding solutions.

Safety with Microbes

WHAT YOU CAN'T SEE CAN HURT YOU

Pathogenic (disease-causing) microorganisms are not appropriate investigation tools in the high school laboratory and should never be used.

Consult with the school nurse to screen students whose immune systems may be compromised by illness or who may be receiving immunosuppressive drug therapy. Such individuals are extraordinarily sensitive to potential infection from generally harmless microorganisms and should not participate in laboratory activities unless permitted to do so by a physician. Do not allow students who have any open cuts, abrasions, or open sores to work with microorganisms.

HOW TO USE ASEPTIC TECHNIQUE

- Demonstrate correct aseptic technique to students prior to conducting a lab activity. Never pipet liquid media by mouth. When possible, use sterile cotton applicator sticks instead of inoculating loops and Bunsen burner flames for culture inoculation. Remember to use appropriate precautions when disposing of cotton applicator sticks: they should be autoclaved or sterilized before disposal.
- Treat all microbes as pathogenic. Seal with tape all petri dishes containing bacterial cultures. Do not use blood agar plates, and never attempt to cultivate microbes from a human or animal source.
- Never dispose of microbe cultures without sterilizing them first. Autoclave or steam-sterilize at 120°C and 15 psi for 15 to 20 minutes all used cultures and any materials that have come in contact with them. If these devices are not available, flood or immerse these articles in full-strength household bleach for 30 minutes, and then discard. Use the autoclave or steam sterilizer yourself; do not allow students to use these devices.
- Wash all lab surfaces with a disinfectant solution before and after handling bacterial cultures.

HOW TO HANDLE BACTERIOLOGICAL SPILLS

- Never allow students to clean up bacteriological spills. Keep on hand a spill kit containing 500 mL of full-strength household bleach, biohazard bags (autoclavable), forceps, and paper towels.
- In the event of a bacterial spill, cover the area with a layer of paper towels. Wet the paper towels with bleach, and allow them to stand for 15 to 20 minutes. Wearing gloves and using forceps, place the residue in the biohazard bag. If broken glass is present, use a brush and dustpan to collect material, and place it in a suitably marked puncture-resistant container for disposal.

Personal Protective Equipment

Chemical goggles (Meeting ANSI Standard Z87.1) These should be worn with any chemical or chemical solution other than water, when heating substances, using any mechanical device, or observing physical processes that could eject an object.

Face shield (Meeting ANSI Standard Z87.1) Use in combination with eye goggles when working with corrosives.

Contact lenses The wearing of contact lenses for cosmetic reasons should be prohibited in the laboratory. If a student must wear contact lenses prescribed by a physician, that student should be instructed to wear eye-cup safety goggles, similar to swimmer's cup goggles, meeting ANSI Standard Z87.1.

Eye-wash station The device must be capable of delivering a copious, gentle flow of water to both eyes for at least 15 minutes. Portable liquid supply devices are not satisfactory and should not be used. A plumbed-in fixture or a perforated spray head on the end of a hose attached to a plumbed-in outlet is suitable if it is designed for use as an eye-wash fountain and meets ANSI Standard Z358.1. It must be within a 30-second walking distance from any spot in the room.

Safety shower (Meeting ANSI Standard Z358.1) Location should be within a 30-second walking distance from any spot in the room. Students should be instructed in the use of the safety shower in the event of a fire or chemical splash on their body that cannot simply be washed off.

Gloves Polyethylene, neoprene rubber, or disposable plastic may be used. Nitrile or butyl rubber gloves are recommended when handling corrosives.

Apron Rubber-coated cloth or vinyl (nylon-coated) halter is recommended.

Student Safety in the Laboratory

Systematic, careful lab work is an essential part of any science program. The equipment and apparatus students will use present various safety hazards. You must be aware of these hazards before students engage in any lab activity. The Teacher Resource Pages at the beginning of each lab in this Lab Manual will guide you in properly directing the equipment use during the experiments. Photocopy the information on the following pages for students. These safety rules always apply in the lab and in the field.

Safety Symbols

The following safety symbols will appear in the instructions for labs and activities to emphasize important notes of caution. Learn what they represent so that you can take the appropriate precautions.

	Eye Protection • Wear approved safety goggles at all times in the lab as directed. • If chemicals get into your eyes, flush your eyes immediately. • Do not wear contact lenses in the lab. • Do not look directly at the sun or any intense light source or laser.
	Hand Safety • Do not cut an object while holding the object in your hand. • Wear appropriate protective gloves when working with an open flame, chemicals, solutions, or wild or unknown plants. • Use a heat-resistant mitt to handle equipment that may be hot.
	Clothing Protection • Wear an apron or lab coat at all times in the lab. • Tie back long hair, secure loose clothing, and remove loose jewelry so that they do not knock over equipment, get caught in moving parts, or come into contact with hazardous materials or electrical connections. • Do not wear open-toed shoes, sandals, or canvas shoes in the lab. • When outside for lab, wear long sleeves, long pants, socks, and closed shoes.
	Glassware Safety • Inspect glassware before use; do not use chipped or cracked glassware. • Use heat-resistant glassware for heating materials or storing hot liquids. • Notify your teacher immediately if a piece of glassware or a light bulb breaks.
	Sharp-Object Safety • Use extreme care when handling all sharp and pointed instruments. • Cut objects on a suitable surface, always in a direction away from your body. • Be aware of sharp objects or edges on equipment or apparatus.
	Chemical Safety • If a chemical gets on your skin, on your clothing, or in your eyes, rinse it immediately (shower, faucet or eyewash fountain) and alert your teacher. • Do not clean up spilled chemicals yourself unless your teacher directs you to do so. • Do not inhale any gas or vapor unless your teacher directs you to do so. • Handle materials that emit vapors or gases in a well-ventilated area.

Safety Symbols continued

	## Electrical Safety • Do not use equipment with frayed electrical cords or loose plugs. • Fasten electrical cords to work surfaces by using tape. • Do not use electrical equipment near water or when clothing or hands are wet. • Hold the plug housing when you plug in or unplug equipment. • Be aware that wire coils in electrical circuits may heat up rapidly.
	## Heating Safety • Be aware of any source of flames, sparks, or heat (such as open flames, heating coils, or hot plates) before working with any flammable substances. • Avoid using open flames. • Know the location of lab fire extinguishers and fire-safety blankets. • Know your school's fire-evacuation routes. • If your clothing catches on fire, walk to the lab shower to put out the fire. • Never leave a hot plate unattended while it is turned on or while it is cooling. • Use tongs or appropriate insulated holders when handling heated objects. • Allow all equipment to cool before storing it.
	## Plant Safety • Do not eat any part of a plant or plant seed. • When outside, do not pick any wild plants unless your teacher instructs you to do so. • Wash your hands thoroughly after handling any part of a plant.
	## Animal Safety • Handle animals only as your teacher directs. • Treat animals carefully and respectfully. • Wash your hands thoroughly after handling any animal.
	## Proper Waste Disposal • Clean and sanitize all work surfaces and personal protective equipment after each lab period as directed by your teacher. • Dispose of hazardous materials only as directed by your teacher. • Dispose of sharp objects (such as broken glass) in the appropriate sharps or broken glass container as directed by your teacher.
	## Hygienic Care • Keep your hands away from your face while you are working on any activity. • Wash your hands thoroughly before you leave the lab or after any activity. • Remove contaminated clothing immediately.

Safety in the Laboratory

1. **Always wear a lab apron and safety goggles.** Wear these safety devices whenever you are in the lab, not just when you are working on an experiment.

2. **No contact lenses in the lab.** Contact lenses should not be worn during any investigations in which you are using chemicals (even if you are wearing goggles). In the event of an accident, chemicals can get behind contact lenses and cause serious damage before the lenses can be removed. If your doctor requires that you wear contact lenses instead of glasses, you should wear eye-cup safety goggles in the lab. Ask your doctor or your teacher how to use this very important and special eye protection.

3. **Personal apparel should be appropriate for laboratory work.** On lab days, avoid wearing long necklaces, dangling bracelets, bulky jewelry, and bulky or loose-fitting clothing. Long hair should be tied back. Loose, flopping, or dangling items may get caught in moving parts, accidentally contact electrical connections, or interfere with the investigation in some potentially hazardous manner. In addition, chemical fumes may react with some jewelry, such as pearls, and ruin them. Cotton clothing is preferable to wool, nylon, or polyesters. Wear shoes that will protect your feet from chemical spills and falling objects— no open-toed shoes or sandals and no shoes with woven leather straps.

4. **NEVER work alone in the laboratory.** Work in the lab only while supervised by your teacher. Do not leave equipment unattended while it is in operation.

5. **Only books and notebooks needed for the activity should be in the lab.** Only the lab notebook and perhaps the textbook should be used. Keep other books, backpacks, purses, and similar items in your desk, locker, or designated storage area.

6. **Read the entire activity before entering the lab.** Your teacher will review any applicable safety precautions before you begin the lab activity. If you are not sure of something, ask your teacher about it.

7. Always heed safety symbols and cautions in the instructions for the experiments, in handouts, and on posters in the room, and always heed cautions given verbally by your teacher. They are provided for your safety.

8. Know the proper fire drill procedures and the locations of fire exits and emergency equipment. Make sure you know the procedures to follow in case of a fire or other emergency.

9. **If your clothing catches on fire, do not run;** WALK to the safety shower, stand under the showerhead, and turn the water on. Call to your teacher while you do this.

10. **Report all accidents to the teacher** IMMEDIATELY, no matter how minor. In addition, if you get a headache or feel ill or dizzy, tell your teacher immediately.

Safety in the Laboratory continued

11. **Report all spills to your teacher immediately.** Call your teacher, rather than cleaning a spill yourself. Your teacher will tell you if it is safe for you to clean up the spill. If it is not safe for you to clean up the spill, your teacher will know how the spill should be cleaned up safely.

12. If a lab directs you to design your own experiments, procedures must be approved by your teacher BEFORE you begin work.

13. DO NOT perform unauthorized experiments or use equipment or apparatus in a manner for which they were not intended. Use only materials and equipment listed in the activity equipment list or authorized by your teacher. Steps in a procedure should only be performed as described in the lab manual or as approved by your teacher.

14. **Stay alert while in the lab, and proceed with caution.** Be aware of others near you or your equipment when you are proceeding with the experiment. If you are not sure of how to proceed, ask your teacher for help.

15. **Horseplay in the lab is very dangerous.** Laboratory equipment and apparatus are not toys; never play in the lab or use lab time or equipment for anything other than their intended purpose.

16. Food, beverages, and chewing gum are NEVER permitted in the laboratory.

17. **NEVER taste chemicals.** Do not touch chemicals or allow them to contact areas of bare skin.

18. **Use extreme CAUTION when working with hot plates or other heating devices.** Keep your head, hands, hair, and clothing away from the flame or heating area, and turn the devices off when they are not in use. Remember that metal surfaces connected to the heated area will become hot by conduction. Gas burners should be lit only with a spark lighter. Make sure all heating devices and gas valves are turned off before leaving the laboratory. Never leave a hot plate or other heating device unattended when it is in use. Remember that many metal, ceramic, and glass items do not always look hot when they are heated. Allow all items to cool before storing them.

19. **Exercise caution when working with electrical equipment.** Do not use electrical equipment that has frayed or twisted wires. Be sure your hands are dry before you use electrical equipment. Do not let electrical cords dangle from work stations; dangling cords can cause tripping or electrical shocks.

20. **Keep work areas and apparatus clean and neat.** Always clean up any clutter made during the course of lab work, rearrange apparatus in an orderly manner, and report any damaged or missing items.

21. Always thoroughly wash your hands with soap and water at the conclusion of each investigation.

Safety in the Field

Activities conducted outdoors require some advance planning to ensure a safe environment. The following general guidelines should be followed for fieldwork.

1. **Know your mission.** Your teacher will tell you the goal of the field trip in advance. Be sure to have your permission slip approved before the trip, and check to be sure that you have all necessary supplies for the day's activity.

2. **Find out about on-site hazards before setting out.** Determine whether poisonous plants or dangerous animals are likely to be present where you are going. Know how to identify these hazards. Find out about other hazards, such as steep or slippery terrain.

3. **Wear protective clothing.** Dress in a manner that will keep you warm, comfortable, and dry. Decide in advance whether you will need sunglasses, a hat, gloves, boots, or rain gear to suit the terrain and local weather conditions.

4. **Do not approach or touch wild animals.** If you see a threatening animal, call your teacher immediately. Avoid any living thing that may sting, bite, scratch, or otherwise cause injury.

5. **Do not touch wild plants or pick wildflowers unless specifically instructed to do so** by your teacher. Many wild plants can be irritating or toxic. Never taste any wild plant.

6. **Do not wander away from others.** Travel with a partner at all times. Stay within an area where you can be seen or heard in case you run into trouble.

7. **Report all hazards or accidents to your teacher immediately.** Even if the incident seems unimportant, let your teacher know what happened.

8. **Maintain the safety of the environment.** Do not remove anything from the field site without your teacher's permission. Stay on trails, when possible, to avoid trampling delicate vegetation. Never leave garbage behind at a field site. Leave natural areas as you found them.

Laboratory Techniques

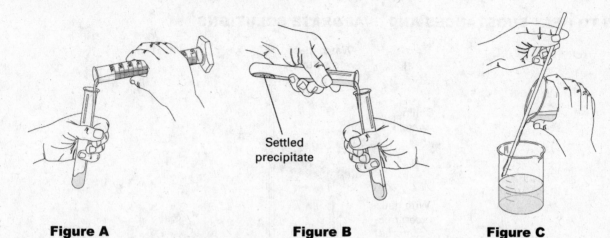

Figure A   Figure B   Figure C

HOW TO DECANT AND TRANSFER LIQUIDS

1. The safest way to transfer a liquid from a graduated cylinder to a test tube is shown in **Figure A**. The liquid is transferred at arm's length, with the elbows slightly bent. This position enables you to see what you are doing while maintaining steady control of the equipment.

2. Sometimes, liquids contain particles of insoluble solids that sink to the bottom of a test tube or beaker. Use one of the methods shown above to separate a supernatant (the clear fluid) from insoluble solids.

   a. **Figure B** shows the proper method of decanting a supernatant liquid from a test tube.

   b. **Figure C** shows the proper method of decanting a supernatant liquid from a beaker by using a stirring rod. The rod should touch the wall of the receiving container. Hold the stirring rod against the lip of the beaker containing the supernatant. As you pour, the liquid will run down the rod and fall into the beaker resting below. When you use this method, the liquid will not run down the side of the beaker from which you are pouring.

Laboratory Techniques continued

HOW TO HEAT SUBSTANCES AND EVAPORATE SOLUTIONS

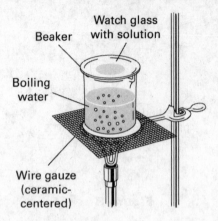

FIGURE D

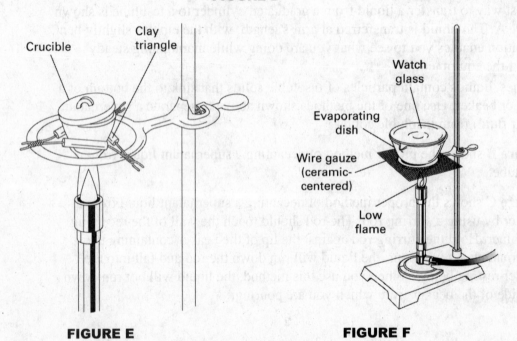

FIGURE E   **FIGURE F**

1. Use care in selecting glassware for high-temperature heating. The glassware should be heat resistant.

2. When heating glassware by using a gas flame, use a ceramic-centered wire gauze to protect glassware from direct contact with the flame. Wire gauzes can withstand extremely high temperatures and will help prevent glassware from breaking.
Figure D shows the proper setup for evaporating a solution over a water bath.

3. In some experiments, you are required to heat a substance to high temperatures in a porcelain crucible. Figure E shows the proper apparatus setup used to accomplish this task.

4. **Figure F** shows the proper setup for evaporating a solution in a porcelain evaporating dish with a watch glass cover that prevents spattering.

Laboratory Techniques continued

5. Glassware, porcelain, and iron rings that have been heated may look cool after they are removed from a heat source, but these items can still burn your skin even after several minutes of cooling. Use tongs, test-tube holders, or heat-resistant mitts and pads whenever you handle these pieces of apparatus.

6. You can test the temperature of beakers, ring stands, wire gauzes, or other pieces of apparatus that have been heated by holding the back of your hand close to their surfaces before grasping them. You will be able to feel any energy as heat generated from the hot surfaces. DO NOT TOUCH THE APPARATUS. Allow plenty of time for the apparatus to cool before handling.

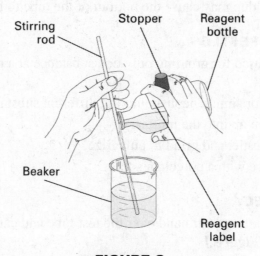

FIGURE G

HOW TO POUR LIQUID FROM A REAGENT BOTTLE

1. Read the label at least three times before using the contents of a reagent bottle.

2. Never lay the stopper of a reagent bottle on the lab table.

3. When pouring a caustic or corrosive liquid into a beaker, use a stirring rod to avoid drips and spills. Hold the stirring rod against the lip of the reagent bottle. Estimate the amount of liquid you need, and pour this amount along the rod, into the beaker. See **Figure G**.

4. Extra precaution should be taken when handling a bottle of acid. Remember the following important rules: Never add water to any concentrated acid, particularly sulfuric acid, because the mixture can splash and will generate a lot of energy as heat. To dilute any acid, add the acid to water in small quantities while stirring slowly. Remember the "triple A's"—*Always Add Acid* to water.

5. Examine the outside of the reagent bottle for any liquid that has dripped down the bottle or spilled on the counter top. Your teacher will show you the proper procedures for cleaning up a chemical spill.

6. Never pour reagents back into stock bottles. At the end of the experiment, your teacher will tell you how to dispose of any excess chemicals.

Laboratory Techniques continued

HOW TO HEAT MATERIAL IN A TEST TUBE

1. Check to see that the test tube is heat resistant.
2. Always use a test tube holder or clamp when heating a test tube.
3. Never point a heated test tube at anyone, because the liquid may splash out of the test tube.
4. Never look down into the test tube while heating it.
5. Heat the test tube from the upper portions of the tube downward, and continuously move the test tube, as shown in **Figure H**. Do not heat any one spot on the test tube. Otherwise, a pressure buildup may cause the bottom of the tube to blow out.

HOW TO USE A MORTAR AND PESTLE

1. A mortar and pestle should be used for grinding only one substance at a time. See **Figure I**.
2. Never use a mortar and pestle for simultaneously mixing different substances.
3. Place the substance to be broken up into the mortar.
4. Pound the substance with the pestle, and grind to pulverize.
5. Remove the powdered substance with a porcelain spoon.

HOW TO DETECT ODORS SAFELY

1. Test for the odor of gases by wafting your hand over the test tube and cautiously sniffing the fumes as shown in **Figure J**.
2. Do not inhale any fumes directly.
3. Use a fume hood whenever poisonous or irritating fumes are present. DO NOT waft and sniff poisonous or irritating fumes.

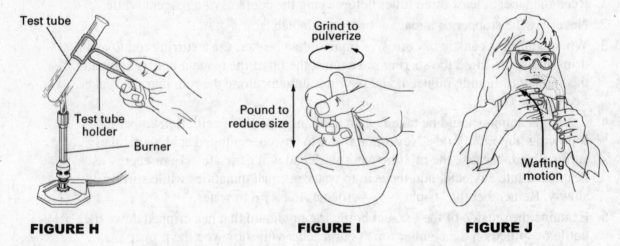

FIGURE H   **FIGURE I**   **FIGURE J**

Student Safety Quiz

Circle the letter of the BEST answer.

1. Before starting an investigation or lab procedure, you should

    a. try an experiment of your own

    b. open all containers and packages

    c. read all directions and make sure you understand them

    d. handle all the equipment to become familiar with it

2. When pouring chemicals between containers, you should hold the containers over

    a. the floor or a waste basket

    b. a fire blanket or an oven mitt

    c. an eyewash station or a water fountain

    d. a sink or your work area

3. If you get hurt or injured in any way, you should

    a. tell your teacher immediately

    b. find bandages or a first aid kit

    c. go to the principal's office

    d. get help after you finish the lab

4. If your glassware is chipped or broken, you should

    a. use it only for solid materials

    b. give it to your teacher

    c. put it back into the storage cabinet

    d. increase the damage so that it is obvious

5. If you have unused chemicals after finishing a procedure, you should

    a. pour them down a sink or drain

    b. mix them all together in a bucket

    c. put them back into their original containers

    d. throw them away where your teacher tells you to

6. If electrical equipment has a frayed cord, you should

   a. unplug the equipment by pulling on the cord

   b. let the cord hang over the side of a counter or table

   c. tell your teacher about the problem immediately

   d. wrap tape around the cord to repair it

7. If you need to determine the odor of a chemical or a solution, you should

   a. use your hand to bring fumes from the container to your nose

   b. bring the container under your nose and inhale deeply

   c. tell your teacher immediately

   d. use odor-sensing equipment

8. When working with materials that might fly into the air and hurt someone's eye, you should wear

   a. goggles

   b. an apron

   c. gloves

   d. a hat

9. Before doing experiments involving a heat source, you should know the location of the

   a. door

   b. windows

   c. fire extinguisher

   d. overhead lights

10. If you get a chemical in your eye, you should

    a. wash your hands immediately

    b. put the lid back on the chemical container

    c. wait to see if your eye becomes irritated

    d. use the eyewash right away

11. When working with a flame or heat source, you should

    a.   tie back long hair or hair that hangs in front of your eyes

    b.   heat substances or objects inside a closed container

    c.   touch an object with your bare hand to see how hot it is

    d.   throw hot objects into the trash when you are done with them

12. As you cut with a knife or other sharp instrument, you should move the instrument

    a.   toward you

    b.   away from you

    c.   vertically

    d.   horizontally

LAB SAFETY QUIZ
Answer Key

1. C	5. D	9. C
2. D	6. C	10. D
3. A	7. A	11. A
4. B	8. A	12. B

Student Safety Contract

Read carefully the Student Safety Contract below. Then, fill in your name in the first blank, date the contract, and sign it.

Student Safety Contract

I will

- read the lab investigation before coming to class
- wear personal protective equipment as directed to protect my eyes, face, hands, and body while conducting class activities
- follow all instructions given by the teacher
- conduct myself in a responsible manner at all times in a laboratory situation

I, _____, have read and agree to abide by the safety regulations as set forth above and any additional printed instructions provided by my teacher or the school district.

I agree to follow all other written and oral instructions given in class.

Signature: _____

Date: _____

QUICK LAB DIRECTED *Inquiry*

How Do Tools that Magnify Help Us Study Cells? GENERAL

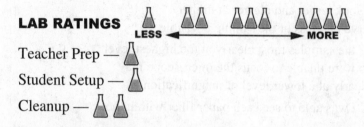

Individual student

30 minutes

LAB RATINGS   LESS ← → MORE

Teacher Prep —

Student Setup —

Cleanup —

MATERIALS

For each student
- cover slips (2)
- eyedropper
- lab apron
- microscope
- microscope slides (2)
- safety goggles
- samples, various
- water

SAFETY INFORMATION

Remind students to review all safety cautions and icons before beginning this lab. Warn students that glass slides and coverslips are fragile, sharp, and break easily.

My Notes

_____

_____

_____

_____

_____

TEACHER NOTES

In this activity, students will make and view microscope slides of samples of various materials. Provide some or all of the following samples for students to choose: letters cut from newspaper, colored yarn or string, feathers, sand, soil, and onion skin. Teach students how to transport and use microscopes before beginning this activity.

Tip This activity may help students understand the history of cell discovery.

Student Tip Some of the characteristics you might include in your descriptions are the object's color, texture, shape, thickness, and orientation.

Skills Focus Practicing Lab Techniques, Making Observations, Comparing Results

MODIFICATION FOR GUIDED *Inquiry*

Provide students with newspaper and the materials to make a new microscope slide. Tell students to use newspaper letters to spell their names or a short message on the slide so that the letters appear correctly when viewed through a microscope.

MODIFICATION FOR INDEPENDENT *Inquiry*

After students have observed their slides, ask them to discuss tips for making microscope slides. For example, students may find that thick samples are hard to see using a microscope. Encourage students to make a list of best practices for slide making. Post this list in the classroom.

Answer Key

4. Answers may vary.

5. Answers may vary.

7. Answers may vary.

8. Answers may vary.
   Teacher Prompt Does the sample appear upside down or backward?

9. Students should understand that samples look larger and clearer at higher magnifications. Some students may observe that less of the sample is visible.

10. Students may indicate that they could see the samples most clearly at the highest level of magnification. However, students who were unable to focus the microscope may indicate that they saw the sample most clearly at a lower level of magnification.

11. Sample answer: At higher magnification, I was able to see each paper fiber within the newspaper sample.
    Teacher Prompt Could you see the whole sample at each level of magnification? If not, why not?

12. Answers may vary.

How Do Tools that Magnify Help Us Study Cells?

In this lab, you will view materials under a microscope to learn how microscopes help us study small objects.

PROCEDURE

1 From your teacher, obtain two different **samples** that you would like to see using a **microscope**.

2 Obtain a clean **microscope slide** and a **cover slip** for each of your samples.

3 To prepare a microscope slide, place a small amount of your sample on the slide; then use an **eyedropper** to place one drop of **water** on the sample. Cover the water and sample with the cover slip.

4 What does the sample on each slide look like without magnification?

_____

_____

5 What do you think each of the samples will look like with magnification?

_____

_____

6 Use a microscope to observe each slide.

7 In the space below, draw what you see **on each slide** at each magnification.

OBJECTIVE
- Compare the appearance of samples at different microscope magnifications.

MATERIALS
For each student
- coverslips (2)
- eyedropper
- lab apron
- microscope
- microscope slides (2)
- safety goggles
- samples, various
- water

Quick Lab continued

8 How do your drawings of the magnified samples compare to what you expected to see in Step 5?

_____

_____

9 Compare your drawings of the same sample at different levels of magnification. How are your drawings alike and different?

_____

_____

_____

10 At which level of magnification can you see the samples most clearly? Explain your answer.

_____

_____

_____

11 How does increasing magnification change what you can see?

_____

_____

12 What other objects would you like to look at using a microscope?

_____

_____

_____

QUICK LAB DIRECTED *Inquiry*

Investigating Cell Size GENERAL

👥 Student pairs
🕐 30 minutes

LAB RATINGS

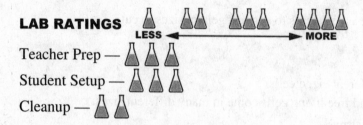

Teacher Prep —

Student Setup —

Cleanup —

MATERIALS

For each pair
- beakers (2)
- calculator
- containers (2)
- craft knife (unless teacher precuts cubes)
- gelatin, prepared
- ruler, metric
- stopwatch (or clock with second hand)
- water, warm

For each student
- lab apron
- safety goggles

SAFETY INFORMATION

Remind students to review all safety cautions and icons before beginning this lab. Students should not hold the craft knife while walking around. Collect the knives from each team after the students have cut their cubes. Advise students to clean up any water that spills. Instruct students to wash and dry their hands after they complete this activity.

TEACHER NOTES

In this activity, students explore one of the constraints that limit cell size, the ratio of cell volume to cell surface area. The student is instructed to obtain two cubes of gelatin, each 3 centimeters (cm) on a side. One of these cubes is then cut into 27 cubes, each 1 cm on a side. The pieces of gelatin represent different-sized cells. Students measure the dimensions of each sized cube. The large, single cube of gelatin is placed in one container; the 27 smaller cubes are placed in a second container. One option is to use 250 mL beakers for the containers. Warm water is added simultaneously to both containers and the timer is started. Students record the time taken for the cubes of gelatin to dissolve. The larger piece takes longer to dissolve even though it represents the same total mass of gelatin as the 27 smaller cubes. Students will use measurements of the original cubes to calculate the cubes' surface area, volume, and the surface area-to-volume ratios. The calculation will show that smaller cubes have higher surface area-to-volume ratios. Students will be asked questions that allow them to use their observations to infer how the surface area-to-volume ratio of a cell would affect the diffusion of materials into the center of a cell.

Prepare gelatin at least one day ahead of class. For best results, use unflavored gelatin and mix with 1/3 the amount of hot water specified in package directions. This will give students a non-sticky, relatively sturdy gelatin sample that will slice easily into defined cubes that will remain intact during handling. It is also recommended that gelatin samples be cold when distributed to students so that as they cut the gelatin, heat from their fingers will not start the melting process. Alternatively, you may wish to precut the cubes before the lesson; this will save time and students will not handle the knives. The water used for the experiment should be warm tap water in the range of 40 °C – 50 °C.

My Notes

_____

_____

_____

_____

_____

Quick Lab continued

Tip Ask students, "Aside from horror movies, why don't we see amoebas the size of elephants?" This activity may help students understand that, due to basic physical constraints, unicellular organisms cannot grow to macroscopic size.

Skills Focus Practicing Lab Techniques, Calculating Ratios, Drawing Conclusions

MODIFICATION FOR GUIDED Inquiry

For the Guided Inquiry option of this activity, ask students to suggest gelatin sizes to cut.

Answer Key

1. Sample answer: The cubes represent different-sized cells.
   Teacher Prompt Cells in our body and free living cells come in many different sizes.

2. 1 cm × 1 cm × 1 cm and 3 cm × 3 cm × 3 cm

5. A sample table with correct answers is shown:

CALCULATED SURFACE AREA, VOLUME, AND SURFACE AREA: VOLUME RATIO

	Surface area (cm²)	Volume (cm³)	SA:V ratio	Average time to dissolve*
3 cm × 3 cm × 3 cm cube	54	27	2	
1 cm × 1 cm × 1 cm cube	6	1	6	

* Accept all reasonable answers.

8. 3 cm × 3 cm × 3 cm cube
   Teacher Prompt Larger objects have larger surface areas and volumes

9. 1 cm × 1 cm × 1 cm cube
   Teacher Prompt Divide the value for the surface area by the value for the volume.

10. Sample answer: The 1 cm × 1 cm × 1 cm cube dissolved faster than the 3 cm × 3 cm × 3 cm cube.
    Teacher Prompt Which size cube has the smaller value in the "Average time to dissolve" column?

11. Sample answer: Because the 1 cm × 1 cm × 1 cm cube dissolved faster than the 3 cm × 3 cm × 3 cm cube, we can infer that materials will diffuse faster into cells with higher surface-to-volume ratios.
    Teacher Prompt Compare how quickly different-sized cubes dissolved. Suppose that materials diffuse into the cell in a way similar to how energy as heat moves into the gelatin.

QUICK LAB DIRECTED *Inquiry*

Investigating Cell Size

In this lab, you will model cells of different sizes to investigate the
physical constraints on cell size.

PROCEDURE

A. BEGIN HERE IF CUBES ARE NOT PRE-CUT

1 Use the craft knife to cut two cubes of gelatin, each measuring
3 cm × 3 cm × 3 cm.

2 Cut one of these cubes into 27 smaller 1 cm × 1 cm × 1 cm cubes.

3 Continue to Step 1, Procedure B.

B. BEGIN HERE IF CUBES ARE PRE-CUT

1 You have one 3 cm × 3 cm × 3 cm gelatin cube and
27 1 cm × 1 cm × 1 cm cubes. What do these cubes represent?

_____

2 Measure the dimensions of one cube of each size using the ruler
to verify their dimensions. Record the dimensions below.

_____

_____

3 Place the single large cube in one of the containers. Place the 27
smaller cubes in the other container.

4 Add the same quantity of warm water to both containers
simultaneously and also be sure that all of the cubes are
submerged in the water. Start the timer.

5 While you wait for the cubes to dissolve, create a table with
columns to record the cubes' dimensions, surface areas,
volumes, and surface area-to-volume ratios.

OBJECTIVES

- Investigate how
surface area-to-
volume ratio
changes with
cell size
- Compare the
ability of different
sized cells to
diffuse water
and nutrients
efficiently.

MATERIALS

For each pair
- beakers (2)
- calculator
- containers (2)
- craft knife
(unless teacher
pre-cuts cubes)
- gelatin, prepared
- ruler, metric
- stopwatch (or clock
with second hand)
- water, warm

For each student
- lab apron
- safety goggles

Quick Lab continued

6 Calculate each size cube's surface area, volume, and surface area-to-volume ratio. Use the averages for the 1 cm cubes from the original measurements. Enter the data into the table.

7 Record the length of time it took for the gelatin cubes to completely dissolve.

8 Which of the cubes had the largest total surface area and largest total volume?

_____

9 Which of the cubes had the highest surface area-to-volume ratio?

_____

10 Which of the cubes dissolved the fastest?

_____

_____

11 From your observations, what can you infer about how the surface area-to-volume ratio of a cell would affect the diffusion of materials into the cell?

_____

_____

EXPLORATION LAB DIRECTED *Inquiry* **AND** GUIDED *Inquiry*

Using A Microscope
To Explore Cells GENERAL

👥 Student pairs

⊕ Two 45-minute class periods

LAB RATINGS

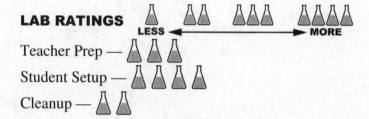

LESS ⟵————⟶ MORE

Teacher Prep —

Student Setup —

Cleanup —

MATERIALS

For each student pair
- cork
- cover slips (3)
- eyedropper
- forceps
- iodine stain
- microscope
- microscope slides (3)
- onion
- pond water

For each student
- lab apron
- safety goggles

SAFETY INFORMATION

Remind students to review all safety cautions and icons before beginning this lab. Students should be cautioned that glass slides and cover slips are breakable and can cause injury when broken. Students should be cautioned to avoid getting iodine on skin or clothing because it stains. Vapors from cutting an onion may irritate eyes.

TEACHER NOTES

In this activity, the student explores three different samples to see how they differ in cellular composition. One of the samples, pond water, will contain mostly free-living organisms. Some of these may be unicellular; others multicellular. If a compound light microscope is available, the students will use a simple stain, iodine, to see if they can detect nuclei in some of the cells. If only a stereo microscope is available, the stain will enable the student to see the variety of cell shapes and sizes. The student will use an identification key to identify organisms in the pond water. The important thing is for the student to recognize that not all unicellular organisms are the same size. Cell size varies greatly among unicellular organisms. And not all microscopic organisms are unicellular. The student will then use the craft knife to cut a thin sliver of cork and stain the cork cells before observing them under the microscope. Finally, the student peels a piece of skin from an onion, stains, and observes these cells under the microscope. Students compare and contrast the cellular makeup of the different samples they observe.

Tip This activity helps the student understand that cell size and shape varies among living things.

Student Tip Look closely at the microorganisms in the pond sample and compare their features with the onion and cork cells.

Skills Focus Practicing Lab Techniques

My Notes

_____

_____

_____

_____

_____

Exploration Lab continued

MODIFICATION FOR INDEPENDENT Inquiry

For the independent inquiry option, have students propose a plan to sample the materials for microscopic examination.

Answer Key for DIRECTED Inquiry

MAKE OBSERVATIONS

6. Accept all reasonable answers.

8. Accept all reasonable answers.

9. Accept all reasonable answers.

10. Accept all reasonable answers.

DRAW CONCLUSIONS

11. Accept all reasonable answers. Answers will vary depending on what students are able to observe.
Teacher Prompt What kinds of structures do you see in the cork and onion samples? Do you see similar structures in the pond water sample?

Connect TO THE ESSENTIAL QUESTION

12. Sample answer: The variety of microorganisms in pond water is much greater than the variety of cells in plant material. Some microorganisms are much smaller than others and some are multicellular. The plant is also multicellular.

Answer Key for GUIDED Inquiry

MAKE A PLAN

2. Accept all reasonable answers.

MAKE OBSERVATIONS

7. Accept all reasonable answers.

9. Accept all reasonable answers.

10. Accept all reasonable answers.

11. Accept all reasonable answers.

Exploration Lab continued

DRAW CONCLUSIONS

12. Accept all reasonable answers. Answers will vary depending on what students are able to observe.

Teacher Prompt What kinds of structures do you see in the cork and onion samples? Do you see similar structures in the pond water sample?

Connect TO THE ESSENTIAL QUESTION

13. Sample answer: The variety of microorganisms in pond water is much greater than the variety of cells in plant material. Some microorganisms are much smaller than others and some are multicellular. The plant is also multicellular.

Name _____ Class _____ Date _____

EXPLORATION LAB **DIRECTED** *Inquiry*

Using A Microscope
To Explore Cells

In this lab you will use a microscope to examine various samples and
describe what you observe. Then you will compare and contrast your
observations of the different samples.

PROCEDURE

ASK A QUESTION

❶ In this lab, you will explore the following questions. What
are similarities and differences between organisms at the cellular
level? Are all cells the same size? Are all single-celled
organisms the same size? What features of plant cells make
them different from single-celled microorganisms?

MAKE OBSERVATIONS

❷ Work with your partner to study microscopic organisms in a
sample of pond water. To do this, make a wet-mount slide.

   a. Use the eyedropper to place 2–3 drops of pond water in the
center of a clean microscope slide.

   b. Put one edge of a cover slip next to the left edge of the drops
of pond water.

   c. Slowly lower the cover slip over the pond water until it is flat on the slide.
If you see air bubbles, pick up the cover slip and try again.

❸ Adjust the objectives of your microscope to choose the lowest magnification.
Place the slide on the microscope stage for viewing. Focus the image using the
following steps.

   a. While looking through the eyepiece at your specimen, slowly focus with the
coarse adjustment knob. This is typically the larger knob. Stop when you see
something come into focus. You may have to move the slide to get an organism
in the field of view.

   b. Switch to the fine adjustment knob (typically the smaller knob) and turn this
until the image becomes clear and in focus.

❹ Carefully switch to an objective with a higher magnification. Do this by
slowly turning the objectives until one with higher magnification snaps into
place. Go through the focusing procedure using the coarse and then fine
adjustment knobs as before. When viewing with the high power objective,
you should focus using the fine adjustment knob only.

OBJECTIVE
• Compare the types
of cells from three
different samples.

MATERIALS
For each student pair
• cork
• cover slips (3)
• eyedropper
• forceps
• iodine stain
• microscope
• microscope
slides (3)
• onion
• pond water
For each student
• lab apron
• safety goggles

Exploration Lab continued

5 Move the slide to find organisms. Look in different areas of the slide for different organisms.

6 Record your observations. Sketch in the table each of the different organisms that you observe. Record any movement of behavior you observe. Include the magnification of the objective lens that you used.

IDENTIFYING ORGANISMS

Organism 1	Organism 2
Magnification used:	Magnification used:
Movement/Behavior:	Movement/Behavior:
Sketch:	Sketch:
Name:	Name:
Organism 3	Organism 4
Magnification used:	Magnification used:
Movement/Behavior:	Movement/Behavior:
Sketch:	Sketch:
Name:	Name:

Exploration Lab continued

7 Use the Identification Key to identify organisms. If an identification cannot be made, write *unknown* in the table.

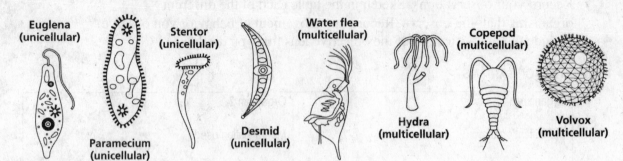

Euglena (unicellular) Stentor (unicellular) Water flea (multicellular) Copepod (multicellular)

Paramecium (unicellular) Desmid (unicellular) Hydra (multicellular) Volvox (multicellular)

8 Use the forceps to peel off a piece of the skin found between layers of onion (this is not the outer skin, but a thin layer inside). Place it on the microscope slide, add a drop of water and a coverslip, and view it through the microscope. Record your observations.

_____

_____

_____

_____

_____

9 Use an eyedropper to place a tiny drop of iodine on the onion. Record your observations, noting any differences between unstained and stained cells.

_____

_____

_____

_____

10 Obtain a thin sliver of cork from your teacher. Place it on the microscope slide. Use the dropper to add iodine stain. View through the microscope. Record your observations.

_____

_____

_____

_____

_____

Exploration Lab continued

DRAW CONCLUSIONS

⓫ **Comparing Samples** Compare your observations for the three samples: pond water, onion skin, and cork. How do your observations differ? Do you notice any similarities between the cork and onion samples?

_____

_____

_____

_____

Connect TO THE ESSENTIAL QUESTION

⓬ **Interpreting Observations** How does the variety of microorganisms in pond water compare with the variety of cells in plant material?

_____

_____

_____

Using A Microscope
To Explore Cells

In this lab you will use a microscope to examine various samples and describe what you observe. Then you will compare and contrast your observations of the different samples.

PROCEDURE

ASK A QUESTION

1 In this lab, you will explore the following questions. What are similarities and differences between organisms at the cellular level? Are all cells the same size? Are all single-celled organisms the same size? What features of plant cells make them different from single-celled microorganisms?

MAKE A PLAN

2 Consider how the samples differ in structure and how they might best be observed with the microscope. Compared with pond water, what is the best way to sample the onion and cork?

_____

_____

_____

OBJECTIVE
• Compare the types of cells from three different samples.

MATERIALS
For each student pair
• cork
• cover slips (3)
• eyedropper
• forceps
• iodine stain
• microscope
• microscope slides (3)
• onion
• pond water
For each student
• lab apron
• safety goggles

MAKE OBSERVATIONS

3 Work with your partner to study microscopic organisms in a sample of pond water. To do this, make a wet-mount slide.

a. Use the eyedropper to place 2–3 drops of pond water in the center of a clean microscope slide.

b. Put one edge of a cover slip next to the left edge of the drops of pond water.

c. Slowly lower the cover slip over the pond water until it is flat on the slide. If you see air bubbles, pick up the cover slip and try again.

4 Adjust the objectives of your microscope to choose the lowest magnification. Place the slide on the microscope stage for viewing. Focus the image using the following steps.

a. While looking through the eyepiece at your specimen, slowly focus with the coarse adjustment knob. This is typically the larger knob. Stop when you see something come into focus. You may have to move the slide in order to get an organism in the field of vision.

b. Switch to the fine adjustment knob (typically the smaller knob) and turn this until the image becomes clear and in focus.

Exploration Lab continued

5 Carefully switch to an objective with a higher magnification. Do this by slowly turning the objectives until the objective with the higher magnification snaps into place. When viewing with the high power objective, you should focus using the fine adjustment knob only.

6 Move the slide to find organisms. Look in different areas of the slide for different organisms.

7 Record your observations. Make a table in your notebook for keeping notes and making sketches of the organisms you see. Record any movement of behavior you observe. Be sure to include the magnification of the objective lens that you used when you are making notes.

8 Use the Identification Key to identify organisms. If an identification cannot be made, record the organism as *unknown* in your notes.

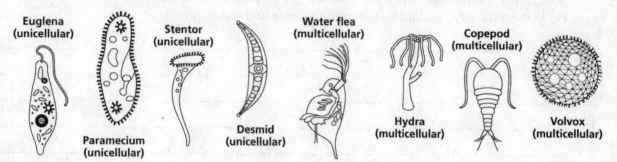

Euglena (unicellular)   Paramecium (unicellular)   Stentor (unicellular)   Desmid (unicellular)   Water flea (multicellular)   Hydra (multicellular)   Copepod (multicellular)   Volvox (multicellular)

9 Using the forceps, peel off a piece of the skin found between layers of onion (this is not the outer skin, but a thin layer inside). Place it on the microscope slide, add a drop of water and a coverslip, and view through the microscope. Record your observations.

_____

_____

_____

_____

10 Use an eyedropper to place a tiny drop of iodine on the onion. Record your observations, noting any differences between unstained and stained cells.

_____

_____

_____

_____

_____

Exploration Lab continued

11 Obtain a thin sliver of cork from your teacher. Place it on the microscope slide. Use the dropper to add iodine stain. After placing the coverslip on the cork, view through the microscope. Record your observations.

_____

_____

_____

_____

DRAW CONCLUSIONS

12 **Comparing Samples** Compare your observations for the three samples: pond water, onion skin, and cork. How do your observations differ? Do you notice any similarities between the cork and onion samples?

_____

_____

_____

_____

_____

Connect TO THE ESSENTIAL QUESTION

13 **Interpreting Observations** How does the variety of microorganisms in pond water compare with the variety of cells in plant material?

_____

_____

_____

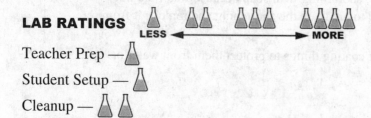

QUICK LAB DIRECTED Inquiry

Analyzing Cell Components BASIC

👥 Small groups
🕑 10 minutes

LAB RATINGS

LESS ←——————→ MORE

Teacher Prep —
Student Setup —
Cleanup —

SAFETY INFORMATION

Remind students to review all safety cautions and icons before beginning this lab. Spilled soap, water, and shortening are all slipping hazards. Advise students to clean up and report all spills immediately.

TEACHER NOTES

In this activity, students will observe how lipids, like those found in shortening, do not mix easily with water. If you do not have a sink in your classroom, you might want to provide students with small dishpans of water to do the experiment at their seats.

Tip This activity may help students understand the hydrophobic nature of lipids.

Skills Focus Making Observations, Drawing Conclusions

MODIFICATION FOR GUIDED Inquiry

Provide students with the materials listed, but do not tell them what procedure to follow. Instead, explain that shortening is oil in solid form. Ask them how they think shortening reacts with water, and if they have ever spilled oil or shortening and tried to clean it up. Tell them to use their materials to determine how to best clean shortening. Discuss class results and how they relate to cell structure.

MODIFICATION FOR INDEPENDENT Inquiry

Ask students what they know about lipids. Remind them that fats and oils are lipids. Challenge students to demonstrate some properties of lipids and to relate those properties to possible roles lipids could play in cells.

MATERIALS

For each group
- cup, clear plastic
- shortening, vegetable
- soap, liquid dishwashing
- water supply or individual pans of water

For each student
- gloves
- lab apron
- safety goggles

My Notes

_____

_____

_____

_____

_____

Answer Key

2. Sample answer: It doesn't work. The water just beads up on the shortening. They don't mix.

3. Sample answer: It's much easier. The soap makes it possible to clean the shortening.

4. Sample answer: It was easier to clean the shortening with soap because water did not dissolve the shortening. The soap helped to break up the shortening and remove it from the cup.

5. Sample answer: They would be good for coating things to protect them from water or to form some sort of enclosure or barrier.

QUICK LAB DIRECTED *Inquiry*

Analyzing Cell Components

Lipids are substances that make up cellular membranes. In this lab, you will observe how lipids, such as shortening, interact with water and soap.

PROCEDURE

❶ Coat the inside of a clear plastic **cup** with **shortening**.

❷ Use **water** to try to clean the shortening out of the cup. Record what happens.

_____

_____

_____

_____

❸ Next, use **soap** and water to try to clean the shortening out of the cup. Record what happens.

_____

_____

_____

_____

❹ Which method was easier for cleaning the shortening? Why do you think that is?

_____

_____

_____

_____

_____

OBJECTIVE

• Explore and describe the nature of lipids.

MATERIALS

For each group
• cup, clear plastic
• shortening, vegetable
• soap, liquid dishwashing
• water supply or individual pans of water

For each student
• gloves
• lab apron
• safety goggles

Quick Lab continued

❺ Given the properties of lipids, what purposes do you think they serve inside living things?

_____

_____

_____

_____

_____

QUICK LAB `DIRECTED` *Inquiry*

Molecules for Life Processes GENERAL

👥 Small groups
🕐 20 minutes

LAB RATINGS

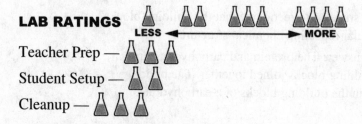

LESS ←————————→ MORE

Teacher Prep —
Student Setup —
Cleanup —

MATERIALS

For each group

- page with polynucleotide structure
- page with polypeptide structure
- page with polysaccharide structure
- page with triacylglyceride structure
- scissors

SAFETY INFORMATION

Remind students to review all safety cautions and icons before beginning this lab. Students should use caution when using scissors.

TEACHER NOTES

Students work in groups to study printed sheets showing the four general types of biomolecules: a polypeptide, a polysaccharide, a polynucleotide, and a triacylglyceride. In their groups, they identify the elements represented (C, H, O, N, P, S) and in which biomolecules these elements are found. Then students cut the biomolecules into monomers and mix them together like a pack of playing cards. They use them to play a game that challenges them to match the monomers to reconstruct each biomolecule. It is best to do this activity after students have learned about the general classes of biomolecules that include proteins, carbohydrates, lipids, and nucleic acids.

The nucleic acid structure does not show carbon and hydrogen atoms in their atomic symbol form. Point this out to students so they have a basic understanding of what the lines represent on this structure.

Tip Photocopy the pages from the Teacher's Edition showing the four sets of biomolecules. Distribute these to students to use for making their playing cards. Alternatively, you can have students copy the drawings onto note cards. If you follow this second option, you must allow extra time beyond the 20 minutes indicated for this activity.

Skills Focus Examining Structures, Recognizing Patterns

MODIFICATION FOR `GUIDED` *Inquiry*

Have students develop their own card game or make a variation of the one described.

My Notes

_____

_____

_____

_____

_____

Answer Key for DIRECTED Inquiry

1. C, H, O, N, P, S

2. C, H, O are present in all of these biomolecules.

3. The protein is the only one to contain sulfur, S. The nucleic acid is the only one to contain phosphorus, P.

9. Accept all reasonable answers. Look for students to recognize that the building blocks within any of the biomolecules have similar repeating chemical structures.

10. Accept all reasonable answers. Sample answer: The protein and carbohydrate are similar in that they are long chains of building blocks joined together. The building blocks of a protein are quite different than the building blocks of a carbohydrate.

QUICK LAB DIRECTED *Inquiry*

Molecules for Life Processes

All living organisms are composed of molecules. In this activity, you will study examples of each major type of molecule found in cells to see how many different elements make up their structures. Then you will cut these large molecules into smaller pieces and play a game that helps you learn to recognize how these smaller pieces combine together to build the much larger molecules cells are made of.

PROCEDURE

1 Obtain one copy of each of the four types of molecules found in living organisms: a protein, a carbohydrate, a lipid, and a nucleic acid. With your group, study each of the four molecular structures. Write down as many different elements as you find represented in the four examples.

_____

_____

_____

2 What element(s) were present in every one of the four examples?

_____

_____

3 What element(s) were present in only one example?

_____

_____

4 Cut the larger molecules along the dotted lines to make a set of rectangles of the same shape and size. Combine all of the rectangles in one group and turn them upside down. Shuffle them as if they were a set of playing cards.

5 Deal the cards one at a time to each member of the group until everyone has four cards. Look at your cards to see if you have enough building blocks to make one biomolecule. If no one has a complete set, you must play until someone does have a complete biomolecule.

Quick Lab continued

6 To play, have the person to the left of the dealer pick one card from any other person's cards. This person looks at the card they chose and decides which card in their hand they want to discard. They pass this card to the person they picked the card from.

7 The next player is to the left of the first player. This person repeats Step 6, choosing a card from anyone in the circle and discarding back to this person.

8 Play continues until one player has at least three building blocks to make one of the four types of biomolecules.

9 What allowed you to decide at any stage of the game whether or not you had structures that could be combined to build a molecule?

_____

_____

10 Choose any two of the biomolecules you worked with in this activity and explain how their chemical structures are similar and how they are different.

_____

_____

_____

_____

Protein

Carbohydrate

Lipid

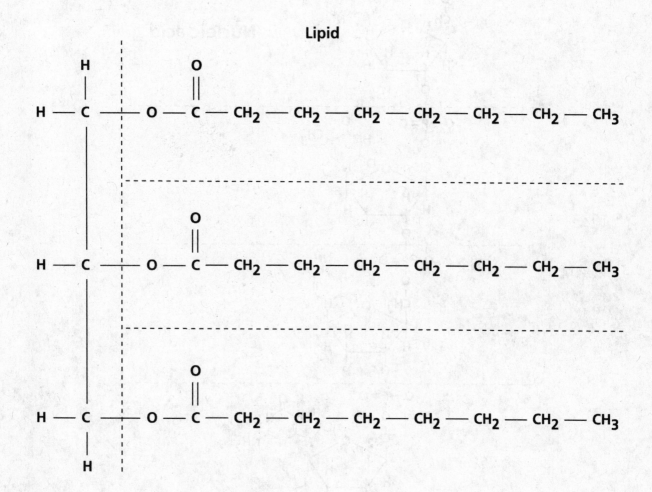

Nucleic acid

QUICK LAB GUIDED *Inquiry*

Comparing Cells GENERAL

👥 Individual student
🕐 30 minutes

LAB RATINGS

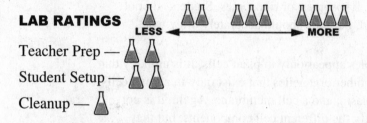

LESS ← → MORE

Teacher Prep —

Student Setup —

Cleanup —

MATERIALS

For each student

- microscope, compound
- paper, blank (1 sheet)
- pencils, colored (optional)
- prepared slide showing animal cells
- prepared slide showing plant cells
- safety goggles

SAFETY INFORMATION

Remind students to review all safety cautions and icons before beginning this lab. Broken microscope slides can cause cuts. Students should immediately report any broken slides.

TEACHER NOTES

In this activity, students will examine animal and plant cells using a microscope, and identify similarities and differences. The plant cells used should have clear cell walls and vacuoles. Leaf cells are ideal. Animal cells should have clear nuclei; muscle cells, cheek cells, or skin cells are ideal. Do not use red blood cell slides as mature red blood cells do not have nuclei and may confuse students. Students should know how to transport, turn on, and focus microscopes before beginning this activity.

Student Tip Be sure to look at and draw the animal cell using the same magnification that you used to look at and draw the plant cell.

Skills Focus Practicing Lab Techniques, Making Observations, Comparing Results

My Notes

_____

_____

_____

_____

_____

MODIFICATION FOR DIRECTED *Inquiry*

Before students examine the cells with the microscope, show them labeled photomicrographs of plant and animal cells that are similar to the ones they will observe. Point out the main differences between the two types of cells, and tell them to look for those features when they examine their own slides.

Answer Key

4. Students' drawings should show cell walls, nuclei, chloroplasts, and vacuoles. They may also be able to identify mitochondria and the cell membrane. Students do not need to accurately identify every cell part, but they should accurately draw what they see.

5. Students' drawings should show nuclei and mitochondria. They may also draw the endoplasmic reticulum, Golgi apparatus, lysosomes, or ribosomes. Students do not need to accurately identify every cell part, but they should accurately draw what they see.

6. Cell walls, chloroplasts, and large vacuoles appear only in plant cells. It is unlikely that students will be able to see centrioles or other organelles that exist only in animal cells. Both types of cells contain nuclei, cytoplasm, and a cell membrane. Again, it is not necessary for students to correctly identify the different cell components, but they should recognize that the cells contain different parts.

7. Students' drawings should contain similar structures. Encourage discussion about the importance of accuracy and its relationship to results.

Comparing Cells

In this lab, you will examine slides of plant cells and animal cells. You will identify similarities and differences between the two types of cells.

PROCEDURE

1 Obtain a prepared **plant cell slide** and a prepared **animal cell slide**.

2 Fold a sheet of **paper** so that you have three wide columns.

3 Label the first column "Plant cell." Label the second column "Both cells." Label the third column "Animal cell."

4 Use a **microscope** to view the plant cell slide. Draw what you see in the first column.

5 Now, use the microscope to view the animal cell slide. Draw what you see in the third column.

6 Below your drawing of the plant cell, draw or list any cell parts that appear in the plant cell but not in the animal cell. Below your drawing of the animal cell, draw or list any cell parts that appear in the animal cell but not in the plant cell. In the middle column, list or draw any cell parts you see that appear in both animal and plant cells.

7 Compare your drawings to the drawings created by your neighbors. Record your observations.

_____

_____

_____

_____

_____

_____

_____

_____

_____

OBJECTIVE

- Compare and contrast animal and plant cells.

MATERIALS

For each student

- microscope, compound
- paper, blank (1 sheet)
- pencils, colored (optional)
- prepared slide showing animal cells
- prepared slide showing plant cells
- safety goggles

QUICK LAB GUIDED *Inquiry*

Making a 3-D Cell Model BASIC

👥 Individual student
🕐 30 minutes

LAB RATINGS

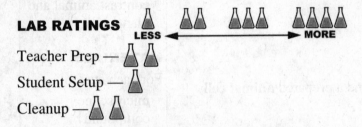

LESS ⟵————————⟶ MORE

Teacher Prep —

Student Setup —

Cleanup —

SAFETY INFORMATION

Remind students to review all safety cautions and icons before beginning this lab. Modeling clay can stain skin and clothing and may irritate some students' skin. Students should wear gloves and an apron when handling modeling clay. Loose objects, such as beans, can pose a slipping hazard if they spill. All spills should be cleaned up immediately.

TEACHER NOTES

In this activity, students will make a cell model. Have a variety of materials that students can use to represent cell parts. You may use whatever materials are available to you.

Skills Focus Making Models

MODIFICATION FOR DIRECTED *Inquiry*

Give students specific ideas about what objects to use to model various cell components. Provide students with labeled diagrams of animal cells to help them construct their models.

MODIFICATION FOR INDEPENDENT *Inquiry*

Have students plan and construct their own animal or plant cell models using any materials they have access to. Students should present their models to the class.

MATERIALS

For each student

- assorted craft supplies, such as yarn/string, balloons, modeling clay, colored paper, beads, glitter, pipe cleaners, dried pasta and beans, and cardboard
- gloves
- glue and/or tape
- lab apron
- pencil
- plastic zip-top bag
- safety goggles
- scissors

My Notes

_____

_____

_____

_____

_____

Quick Lab continued

Answer Key

3. See sample table below.

5. See sample table below.

6. A sample completed table is shown below.

Cell part	Material selected	Reason
cell membrane	zip-top bag	The zip-top bag can be used to contain other materials, just like the cell membrane.
nucleus	balloon with string inside	The nucleus contains DNA, so I've put string (DNA) inside the balloon (nucleus) that separates it from the rest of the cell.
cytoskeleton	pipe cleaners	Some types of cytoskeletons appear long and thin, like the pipe cleaners.
ribosomes	small beads	Ribosomes are small organelles, and the beads are very small compared to the other materials in this "cell."
endoplasmic reticulum	blue modeling clay and beads	I shaped the modeling clay into layers and longer branched pieces. I stuck beads into some parts of the layered clay to represent the rough ER. The longer branched pieces without beads represent the smooth ER.
Golgi complex	green modeling clay	I shaped the modeling clay into layers of folded stacks, just like the Golgi complex.
mitochondria	kidney beans	Mitochondria are kidney bean shaped.
lysosomes	large beads	Lysosomes are larger than ribosomes, so the beads representing lysosomes are larger than the beads representing ribosomes.

8. Accept all reasonable sketches.

Making a 3-D Cell Model

In this lab, you will create a model of an animal cell.

PROCEDURE

❶ Gather a **piece of paper** and various **craft supplies** from your teacher.

❷ Draw a three-column table below. Add rows as needed to the table.

OBJECTIVE

- Create a model of a cell.

MATERIALS

For each student

- assorted craft supplies, such as yarn/string, balloons, modeling clay, colored paper, beads, glitter, pipe cleaners, dried pasta and beans, and cardboard
- gloves
- glue and/or tape
- lab apron
- pencil
- plastic zip-top bag
- safety goggles
- scissors

Quick Lab continued

3 Label the first column "Cell part." In this column, list all of the parts of an animal cell.

4 Label the second column "Material selected."

5 Look at all of the craft materials that are available. Determine which materials you want to use to model each cell part, and list them in your table.

6 Label the third column "Reason." In this column, write the reason you have decided to use each material to represent each cell part.

7 Assemble your cell.

8 Draw a picture of your completed cell model in the space below. Label each cell part.

QUICK LAB **DIRECTED** Inquiry

Cell Walls and Wilting ADVANCED

MATERIALS

For each group
- beaker
- celery stalk with leaves, wilted
- food coloring (a few drops)
- plastic wrap
- spoon
- water (50 mL)

For each student
- gloves
- lab apron
- safety goggles

👥 Small groups

🕐 5 minutes one day, plus 10 minutes the next day

LAB RATINGS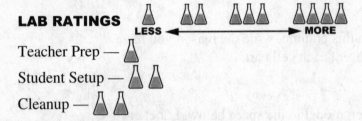

Teacher Prep —

Student Setup —

Cleanup —

SAFETY INFORMATION

Remind students to review all safety cautions and icons before beginning this lab. Food coloring can stain skin and clothing. Students should wear gloves and aprons while handling food coloring. Water can pose a slipping hazard if it spills on the floor. All spills should be wiped up immediately. Remind students not to eat or drink anything in the laboratory.

TEACHER NOTES

In this activity, students will observe the function of organelles that are unique to plant cells such as the cell wall and large central vacuole. Leave the celery out in a dry place the night before the activity to help it wilt. Shortly before the activity, cut the bottom end of each rib. Keep the leaves on the ribs. Transpiration from the leaf surfaces will enhance the uptake of water. The purpose of the color in the water is to show that the water has actually traveled up the rib through the vascular tubes. To a certain extent, color inside the rib can be seen, but consider cutting a rib of celery below the leaves so that color can be seen in the cross sections of the xylem tubes.

Tip Use cold water to achieve optimal results.

Skills Focus Making Observations, Explaining Results, Applying Concepts

My Notes

_____

_____

_____

_____

_____

MODIFICATION FOR INDEPENDENT Inquiry

Have students work in groups to develop an investigation that will allow them to study an aspect of plant structure and function. They should select an aspect of structure-function relationships in plants that they are interested in. Allow them to carry out all reasonable procedures. They should share their results with the class.

Answer Key

2. Answers will vary, but should be close to 50 mL.

3. Sample answer: The celery is wilted. It is soft and easy to bend.

6. Sample answer: The celery is much firmer. It has thin lines of color in its stalk and leaves. It feels much more rigid than it did.

7. Answers will vary, but should be less than 50 mL.

8. Sample answer: The celery became firmer, and the volume of water decreased.

9. Sample answer: The large central vacuole and cell wall make a plant cell rigid. The plant cells became rigid as the celery absorbed the water from the beaker.

QUICK LAB DIRECTED *Inquiry*

Cell Walls and Wilting

In this lab, you will learn how the vacuole and cell wall in plant cells
work together to provide a plant with structure.

PROCEDURE

❶ Add 50 mL **water** to a **beaker.** Add 4–5 drops of **food coloring**,
and stir with a **spoon** until the color is even.

❷ Record the amount of water in the beaker.

_____

❸ Study the stalk of **celery.** Record your observations below.

_____

_____

_____

_____

❹ Place the stalk of celery into the water. Make sure the base of
the celery stalk is in the water.

❺ Leave the setup overnight.

❻ Remove the celery from the water and study it. Record your
observations below.

_____

_____

_____

_____

_____

OBJECTIVE

• Describe the
functions of the
cell wall and water
vacuole in plant
cells.

MATERIALS

For each group

• beaker
• celery stalk with
leaves, wilted
• food coloring
(a few drops)
• plastic wrap
• spoon
• water (50 mL)

For each student

• gloves
• lab apron
• safety goggles

Quick Lab continued

7 Record the volume of water remaining in the beaker.

_____

8 Describe any changes that occurred to the celery and to the volume of the water.

_____

_____

_____

_____

_____

9 Describe how the structure of the plant cell is responsible for the change that you observed.

_____

_____

_____

_____

_____

_____

QUICK LAB DIRECTED Inquiry

Evaluating Specialization GENERAL

👥 Small groups

🕐 20 minutes

LAB RATINGS

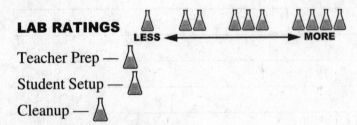

LESS ◄——————► MORE

Teacher Prep —

Student Setup —

Cleanup —

MATERIALS

For each group
• marker
• paper
• pencil
• ruler
• scissors
• tape

For each student
• safety goggles

SAFETY INFORMATION

Remind students to review all safety cautions and icons before beginning this lab. Students should use caution when handling scissors. Paper strips on the floor may be a slipping hazard. All dropped paper should be picked up immediately.

TEACHER NOTES

In this activity, students will make paper chains through multiple steps in order to investigate how specialization affects efficiency. Many of the tasks that are performed in the human body, such as making cell parts, require multiple steps. Students will perform the same activity multiple times to determine how specialization affects the number of paper chain loops they can construct. Students will first work on their own, performing all the tasks of the activity as unicellular organisms do. Then, students will work within a group and perform only a single specialized task, as the cells of multicellular organisms do.

Students will perform tasks for only 5 minutes. When students are counting chain loops, be sure they only include loops that are completely finished and connected in a chain after time is up.

Skills Focus Applying Concepts, Evaluating Procedures

MODIFICATION FOR GUIDED Inquiry

Instead of telling students the steps to make paper chain loops, provide them with the materials and ask them to develop their own procedure. Their goal should be to maximize efficiency within a given timeframe. With teacher approval, have students carry out their procedures and record how many paper chain loops they made. Then, instruct students to form groups and evaluate and compare each other's methods and results. Students should coordinate their efforts and develop a new group procedure to maximize efficiency. They should discover that assigning one task per student, or more than one student to the most time consuming tasks, improves efficiency. Students should turn in their procedures and results, and answer Questions 8 and 9 on the student worksheet.

My Notes

_____

_____

_____

_____

_____

Quick Lab continued

MODIFICATION FOR INDEPENDENT *Inquiry*

Students should devise their own investigation to evaluate specialized versus non-specialized processes. They may do a research report or design an experiment. They should create a procedure or outline, including all materials and resources, as well as a method for recording data and reporting results. With approval, they should carry out their research or experiments and present their conclusions as a lab report.

Answer Key

3. Answers will vary.

4. Answers will vary.

5. Sample answer: It takes a long time to write the alphabet on the paper strip. If two people work on that step, we can get it done more quickly. We will also assign different tasks to each student so that once the first loop is made, we can work on multiple tasks at once.

6. Answers will vary.

7. Sample answer: working with in a group

8. Sample answer: Working alone is like being a unicellular organism that has to perform all its functions by itself. Working in a group is like a multicellular organism, where some cells can specialize and perform certain functions.

Evaluating Specialization

In this activity, you will build a paper chain according to specific steps to explore the advantages of specialization. Many of the tasks that are performed in the human body require multiple steps. Different cells may perform different steps in the process. In this activity, you will first build the chain alone, performing all the steps yourself. Then you will coordinate with a group to build the chain, dividing the steps among the group members, with each one specializing in only one function. You will then evaluate the efficiency and productivity of working alone versus working within a group. You will compare this activity to the hierarchical organization of organisms, from cells to organisms.

PROCEDURE

1 Review the following instructions for constructing a paper chain:

A. Use a **ruler** and **pencil** to mark strips on a sheet of **paper** that are 8 inches long and 1 inch wide.

B. Use **scissors** to carefully cut out each strip.

C. Use a **marker** to write the entire alphabet on each strip.

D. Make the first loop in the chain by curling the strip end to end and using **tape** to connect the ends and make a loop.

E. For the rest of the strips, thread one end of the strip through the previous loop, and tape the ends of the strip to form another loop.

2 Gather your materials.

3 When your teacher instructs you to begin, make as many loops in your paper chain as you can within 5 minutes. When time is up, count how many loops you have made and record the number below.

_____

4 Form a group with four other students. Add up all the chain loops you each made. What is the total number of paper chain loops made by your group working as individuals?

_____

OBJECTIVES

• Evaluate the advantages of specialization.

• Compare models of unicellular and multicellular processes.

MATERIALS

For each group
• marker
• paper
• pencil
• ruler
• scissors
• tape
For each student
• safety goggles

Quick Lab continued

5 With your group, discuss how you could work together to make more paper chain loops in 5 minutes. Do any steps of the paper chain process take a long time? How can you make this step more efficient? How will you organize your group to make more loops?

_____

_____

_____

_____

_____

_____

6 When your teacher says to begin, work with your group to make paper chain loops for 5 minutes. How many paper chain loops did your group make?

_____

7 Did you make more paper chain loops when you were working individually or when you were working with your group?

_____

_____

_____

8 How does working alone versus working in a group relate to specialization in unicellular versus multicellular organisms?

_____

_____

_____

_____

_____

_____

_____

9 If you have time, repeat Steps 4–6 and try to improve your efficiency.

QUICK LAB DIRECTED Inquiry

Observing Plant Organs GENERAL

👥 Individual student

🕐 40 minutes

LAB RATINGS

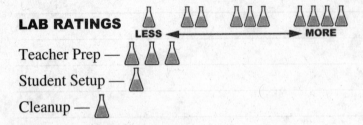

LESS ⟵————⟶ MORE

Teacher Prep —

Student Setup —

Cleanup —

MATERIALS

For each student

- carrot
- colored pencils
- hand lens
- knife
- microscope
- prepared carrot slide
- reference materials
- safety goggles

SAFETY INFORMATION

Remind students to review all safety cautions and icons before beginning this lab. Students should use extreme caution while cutting the carrot in half. Although the carrots would be safe for students to ingest, remind them that they should never eat foods used in laboratory explorations.

TEACHER NOTES

In this activity, students will observe a carrot to learn more about the structure and function of a taproot system. Before beginning this lab, prepare carrot slides for each student. Use a single-edged razor blade to cut a *very thin* slice of the carrot. Carefully place the carrot section on the slide. Wear plastic gloves and a lab apron for the next steps. Use a dropper to cover the carrot with methylene blue stain. Let the stain set for one minute before pouring alcohol over the carrot until no more stain washes off. Cover the carrot with another slide.

Teacher Tip Review how to use a microscope before beginning this lab.

Skills Focus Practicing Lab Techniques, Making Observations, Making Inferences

MODIFICATION FOR INDEPENDENT Inquiry

Have students ask a question about plant organs and develop a hypothesis to answer their question. The students will then design a procedure to test their hypothesis. Allow students to carry out all safe and reasonable procedures and have them share their findings with the class.

My Notes

_____

_____

_____

_____

_____

Answer Key

1. Accept all reasonable drawings.
   Teacher Prompt Suggest that if students know the names of root structures, they should label them.

2. Accept all reasonable drawings.
   Teacher Prompt Suggest that if students know the names of root structures, they should label them.

3. Sample answer: Hair on the root increases surface area, which means the plant can absorb more water. Inside the root are tubes that carry nutrients to the stem and leaves.

4. Sample answer: To anchor the plant in the soil

5. Accept all reasonable diagrams and paragraphs explaining an animal's digestive or excretory system.

QUICK LAB DIRECTED *Inquiry*

Observing Plant Organs

Cells that have similar functions make up tissues, and tissues with similar functions make up organs and organ systems. Organ systems have specialized jobs within an organism. The root is a plant organ whose job is to obtain nutrients for the plant. Animals also have organs they use to obtain nutrients. In this lab, you will observe the taproot system of a carrot plant. Then you will choose an animal organ system that has a similar function and draw a picture of it and write a short explanation of its function.

PROCEDURE

1 Use a **hand lens** to observe the **taproot** of a carrot plant. Draw what you see. Cut the carrot in half lengthwise with the **knife** and draw what you see.

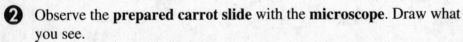

2 Observe the **prepared carrot slide** with the **microscope**. Draw what you see.

OBJECTIVES

- Observe and describe the root system of a plant.
- Describe an animal organ system.

MATERIALS

For each student
- carrot
- colored pencils
- hand lens
- knife
- microscope
- prepared carrot slide
- reference materials
- safety goggles

Quick Lab continued

❸ What features of a root would help it get nutrients for the plant?

_____

_____

_____

❹ Can you think of another function of the root?

_____

_____

_____

❺ Pick an animal that might eat the carrot. Which organ system helps the animal get nutrients from food? Use **reference materials** to find out. Then write a short paragraph explaining how the organ system works. Draw a picture of the organ system.

_____

_____

_____

_____

_____

EXPLORATION LAB DIRECTED Inquiry OR GUIDED Inquiry

The Organization of Organisms GENERAL

MATERIALS

For each pair
- colored pencils
- light microscope
- paper, white
- poster board, white
- prepared microscope slide showing a specific type of tissue
- ruler

For each student
- safety goggles

🖧 Student pairs

🕐 45 minutes

LAB RATINGS

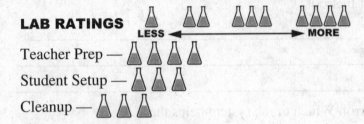

LESS ⟵——————⟶ MORE

Teacher Prep —

Student Setup —

Cleanup —

SAFETY INFORMATION

Remind students to review all safety cautions and icons before beginning this lab. Caution students to use care when handling glass slides. Remind students to begin viewing the slides on the lowest power objective lens. Instruct students to return slides to their storage containers as soon as they are finished using them and to wash their hands after handling the slides.

TEACHER NOTES

In this lab, students will observe and describe the hierarchical organization of organisms, from cells to tissues to organs to organ systems to organisms. Review with students the proper way to use a microscope. Warn students that slides are very fragile and have sharp edges. If slides and microscopes are unavailable, you may provide students with color photographs of cells and tissues.

   To prepare for this lab, set out a sample of prepared microscope slides with various plant tissues, such as leaf epidermis and root tip, and various animal tissues, such as blood and muscle tissue. Tissue from any organism will work, as long as individual cells are visible. Label each slide with the organism and type of tissue.

Skills Focus Organizing Results, Making Models, Describing Patterns

My Notes

_____

_____

_____

_____

_____

MODIFICATION FOR INDEPENDENT Inquiry

Supply live plants from which students may prepare tissue samples, scalpels, slides, cover slips, and stain. Guide students in the procedures of slide preparation. Caution students to be careful while cutting plant parts. Encourage students to view tissue samples from several different organs in the plant. Ask students to form hypotheses about the structure and function of different cells and tissues within the plant. Have students plan and carry out an experiment to test one of their hypotheses.

Exploration Lab continued

Answer Key for DIRECTED Inquiry

MAKE OBSERVATIONS

2. Answers will vary.

3. Answers will vary.

4. Students' drawings should show the different components of the cell, as well as the overall shape of the cell.

5. Students' drawings should clearly show how the cells in the tissue are arranged to make up the tissue.

RESEARCH A PROBLEM

6. Answers will vary.

BUILD A MODEL

8. Students' posters should show that cells make up tissues, tissues make up organs, organs make up organ systems, and organ systems make up organisms.

ANALYZE THE RESULTS

9. Sample answer: The structure and types of cells, tissues, and organs are different from one organism to another, but the overall pattern of hierarchical organization is similar.

10. Accept all reasonable responses.

DRAW CONCLUSIONS

11. Sample answer: Many systems in nature have a hierarchical structure, including all multicellular organisms, ecosystems, planets, and solar systems.

Connect TO THE ESSENTIAL QUESTION

12. Sample answer: Yes, all living things are based on the cell as the fundamental unit of life. Cells are organized into tissues, tissues into organs, and organs into organ systems in all multicellular plants and animals.

Answer Key for GUIDED Inquiry

ASK A QUESTION

2. Answers will vary.

FORM A PREDICTION

3. Answers will vary.

TEST THE PREDICTION

4. Answers will vary.

Exploration Lab continued

MAKE OBSERVATIONS

5. Students' drawings should show the different components of the cell, as well as the overall shape of the cell.

6. Students' drawings should clearly show how the cells in the tissue are arranged to make up the tissue.

BUILD A MODEL

9. Students' posters should show that cells make up tissues, tissues make up organs, organs make up organ systems, and organ systems make up organisms.

ANALYZE THE RESULTS

10. Sample answer: Cells in a root tip each take in water across their membranes, which helps the root perform the function of taking in water for a plant.

DRAW CONCLUSIONS

11. Sample answer: Most multicellular organisms are made up of many different kinds of cells, tissues, and organs. The diagram has only enough space to show one type of cell, tissue, organ, etc.

12. Answers will vary.

Connect TO THE ESSENTIAL QUESTION

13. Sample answer: Yes, all living things are based on the cell as the fundamental unit of life. Cells are organized into tissues, tissues into organs, and organs into organ systems in all multicellular plants and animals.

EXPLORATION LAB `DIRECTED` *Inquiry*

The Organization of Organisms

In this lab, you will observe how tissues are made up of cells. You will use drawings and images to create a diagram that shows the hierarchical organization of an organism from cell to tissue to organ to organ system to organism.

PROCEDURE

ASK A QUESTION

❶ In this lab, you will investigate the following question: How are organisms organized?

MAKE OBSERVATIONS

❷ Choose one of the **prepared microscope slides** provided by your teacher. The slide will contain a sample of tissue from an organism. Write the name of the organism and the type of tissue on the lines below.

_____

_____

❸ Set your **microscope** to the lowest power objective lens. Place your slide on the microscope tray. Focus on the tissue, and describe what you observe.

_____

_____

_____

_____

❹ On a piece of **white paper**, make a drawing of a single cell. Try to make your drawing as accurate as possible. You may switch to a higher-powered objective lens to see more detail.

OBJECTIVE
• Describe the hierarchical organization of organisms, from cells to tissues to organs to organ systems to organisms.

MATERIALS
For each pair
• colored pencils
• light microscope
• paper, white
• poster board, white
• prepared microscope slide showing a specific type of tissue
• ruler
For each student
• safety goggles

Exploration Lab continued

5 On the same paper, make a drawing of the tissue sample as a whole. You may switch back to a lower-powered objective lens. Your drawing should show how the cells fit together to form the tissue.

RESEARCH A PROBLEM

6 Use the Internet or library resources to research the hierarchical organization of your organism, from organ to organ system to organism. Find out which organ contains the tissue you observed, and which organ system or systems contain the organ. Complete the chart below with a description of each level of organization for your organism, beginning with the cell and tissue types you observed.

ORGANIZATION OF YOUR ORGANISM

Cell	Tissue	Organ	Organ System	Organism

7 Find photographs, drawings, or diagrams representing the organ, one of the organ systems that contain the organ, and the organism itself. List your sources below.

_____

_____

_____

_____

BUILD A MODEL

8 Use your drawings and images from your research to create a diagram showing the hierarchical organization of your organism. Arrange your images on the **poster board** provided by your teacher. Use arrows to show the order of organization from smallest to largest. Display your poster in the classroom.

Exploration Lab continued

ANALYZE THE RESULTS

9 **Comparing Observations** Study the posters of other students. In what ways do the details of the levels of organization differ? In what ways are they similar?

_____

_____

_____

_____

10 **Developing Concepts** Your diagram represents one strand of organization within your organism. How many different diagrams do you think could be made for your organism? Explain your answer.

_____

_____

_____

_____

DRAW CONCLUSIONS

11 **Describing Patterns** How can understanding the pattern of hierarchical organization help you learn more about nature?

_____

_____

_____

_____

Connect TO THE ESSENTIAL QUESTION

12 **Recognizing Patterns** Do all multicellular organisms follow the same pattern of organization? Explain.

_____

_____

_____

_____

EXPLORATION LAB GUIDED *Inquiry*

The Organization of Organisms

In this lab, you will observe how tissues are made up of cells. You will use drawings and images to create a diagram that shows the hierarchical organization of an organism from cell to tissue to organ to organ system to organism.

PROCEDURE

ASK A QUESTION

1 In this lab, you will investigate the following question: How are organisms organized?

2 Choose one of the **prepared microscope slides** provided by your teacher. The slide will contain a sample of tissue from an organism. Write the name of the organism and the type of tissue on the lines below.

_____

_____

FORM A PREDICTION

3 Based on what you know about tissues, predict what you will observe on the slide.

_____

_____

_____

TEST THE PREDICTION

4 Set your **microscope** to the lowest power objective lens. Place your slide on the microscope tray. Focus on the tissue, and describe what you observe.

_____

_____

_____

_____

OBJECTIVE

• Describe the hierarchical organization of organisms, from cells to tissues to organs to organ systems to organisms.

MATERIALS

For each pair

• colored pencils
• light microscope
• paper, white
• poster board, white
• prepared microscope slide showing a specific type of tissue
• ruler

For each student

• safety goggles

Exploration Lab continued

MAKE OBSERVATIONS

5 On a piece of **white paper**, make a drawing of a single cell. Try to make your drawing as accurate as possible. You may switch to a higher-powered objective lens to see more detail.

6 On the same paper, make a drawing of the whole tissue sample. You may switch back to a lower-powered objective lens.

RESEARCH A PROBLEM

7 Use the Internet or library resources to research the hierarchical organization of your organism, from organ to organ system to organism. Find out which organ contains the tissue you observed, and which organ system or systems contain that organ. Record your notes and sources below.

_____

_____

_____

_____

_____

_____

_____

_____

Exploration Lab continued

8 Find photographs, drawings, or diagrams representing the organ, one of the organ systems that contain the organ, and the organism itself.

BUILD A MODEL

9 Use your drawings and images from your research to create a diagram showing the hierarchical organization of your organism. Display your diagram in the classroom.

ANALYZE THE RESULTS

10 **Organizing Concepts** Explain how at each level of organization the smaller parts that make up that level work together to perform necessary life functions. In your response, discuss specific examples from your diagram.

_____

_____

_____

_____

_____

_____

_____

_____

_____

DRAW CONCLUSIONS

11 **Recognizing Constraints** Your diagram shows one strand of organization within your organism. Discuss how this compares to the actual structure and function of your organism, and explain the limitations of the diagram.

_____

_____

_____

_____

_____

Exploration Lab continued

⑫ Constructing Models Plan another type of model that shows the levels of organization in an organism. Compare the limitations of your new model with the diagram you created.

_____

_____

_____

_____

_____

_____

_____

Connect TO THE ESSENTIAL QUESTION

⑬ Recognizing Patterns Do all multicellular organisms follow the same pattern of organization? Explain.

_____

_____

_____

_____

QUICK LAB GUIDED Inquiry

Investigate Microorganisms BASIC

👥 Student pairs

🕐 25 minutes

LAB RATINGS

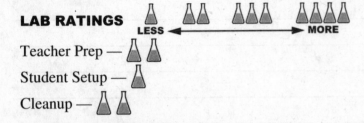

LESS ← → MORE

Teacher Prep —

Student Setup —

Cleanup —

MATERIALS

For each pair
- *Daphnia* culture
- depression microscope slides, with cover slips (2)
- eyedropper
- hydra culture
- lamp or flashlight
- microscope
- water, cold
- water, warm

For each student
- safety goggles

SAFETY INFORMATION

Remind students to review all safety cautions and icons before beginning this lab. Students should exercise caution and care when working with the microscopes, slides, and cultures.

TEACHER NOTES

In this activity, students will observe how microorganisms react to external stimuli such as light, temperature changes, and other organisms.

Tip Remind students that microorganisms do not "see" their world in the same way we do so they must think broadly when evaluating how microorganisms interact with their environment. A stereo microscope will work best for this activity. If flat slides are used, the teacher should not have any coverslips available because if a coverslip is used, the movement of the organisms will be compromised. The students should make sure that the drop of solution on the slide with the organism(s) in it is large enough for them to maintain mobility. The students may have to watch the hydra for a couple of minutes to notice movement, but the *Daphnia* are very active. Since the hydra are slow moving (they may even see them somersault), when they add the *Daphnia* to the slide, the students should be focused on a hydra. The active *Daphnia* will move into the area and get stung by the nematocysts on the hydra's appendages. Remind students that most microscopes have an adjustable stage light which can be turned up and down.

Student Tip Keep in mind that the basic requirements of life apply to microorganisms even though some of the resources these organisms use are dramatically different from what we humans use.

Skills Focus Identifying Variables, Making Observations, Drawing Conclusions

MODIFICATION FOR INDEPENDENT Inquiry

Provide students with the question and materials for this activity and allow them to design and run their own experiments, record observations, and draw conclusions on their own.

My Notes

_____

_____

_____

_____

_____

Answer Key

2. Accept all reasonable answers.

3. Accept all reasonable answers. Drawings should illustrate the hydra's long body and thin appendages.

4. The hydra contracts in response to light.

5. The hydra move away from cold water.

6. The hydra moves away from warm water.

7. Accept all reasonable answers.

8. Hydras and *Daphnia* have a predator-prey relationship.

Investigate Microorganisms

In this activity, you will observe the behavior of microorganisms under different environmental conditions.

PROCEDURE

① The question you will be exploring in this lab is: How do microorganisms respond to various stimuli in their environment?

② You will have two different microorganism cultures to investigate. Work with your partner to decide how you will test one of these, the hydra, for their response to light, cold, and warmth. Write your plan below.

_____

_____

_____

③ Place a drop of hydra culture on a microscope slide. Use your microscope to view the sample. Make a sketch of your observations.

④ Test the hydra for response to light. What do you observe?

_____

_____

⑤ Test the hydra for response to cold by replacing the water on the slide with cold water. What do you observe?

_____

_____

OBJECTIVE
• Observe how microorganisms respond to changes in their environment.

MATERIALS
For each pair
• *Daphnia* culture
• depression microscope slides, with cover slips (2)
• eyedropper
• hydra culture
• lamp or flashlight
• microscope
• water, cold
• water, warm
For each student
• safety goggles

Quick Lab continued

6 Test the hydra for response to warmth by replacing the water on the slide with warm water. What do you observe?

_____

_____

7 Now add a drop of *Daphnia* culture to the hydra on the slide. Observe the combined sample under the microscope. Make a sketch of the *Daphnia*.

8 Observe how the hydra and *Daphnia* react to one another. What do you conclude about their relationship?

_____

_____

QUICK LAB INDEPENDENT Inquiry

Homeostasis and Adaptations BASIC

👥 Small groups
⏲ 30 minutes

LAB RATINGS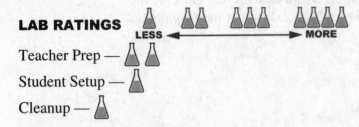

LESS ◄──────► MORE

Teacher Prep —

Student Setup —

Cleanup —

MATERIALS
For each group
• camera (optional)
• journal
• pencil or pen

My Notes

_____
_____
_____
_____
_____

SAFETY INFORMATION

Remind students to review all safety cautions and icons before beginning this lab. Have students work in teams while moving about to gather information on tree leaf adaptation. Be sure that students properly dispose of their leaves after they have completed their observations.

TEACHER NOTES

All living things have a need to maintain homeostasis. In this activity, students will discover how the physical characteristics of organisms relate to the environment in which they live by observing and analyzing the differing characteristics of deciduous and coniferous tree leaves.

Tip Have students extend the exercise to humans. To what extent do we change in response to our own environment to maintain homeostasis? What conditions are we able to respond to? Are there limits to those responses?

Student Tip What do leaves do for trees, and what resources do they need to do it?

Skills Focus Making Observations, Applying Concepts

MODIFICATION FOR GUIDED Inquiry

Define the term *homeostasis*, then assist students with restating that definition in their own terms, highlighting the resources that organisms need to stay alive and the fact that maintaining homeostasis requires energy (shivering is an excellent example of this). Once students have a list of needs, have them use that list as a lens through which to interpret characteristics of deciduous versus coniferous tree leaves.

Answer Key

3. Sample answer: Deciduous leaves are flat and broad, with different colors and textures on the top and bottom, while coniferous "leaves" are thin, long, and the same on all sides.

4. Sample answer: The conifers tend to be relatively short trees and have leaves along the length of the branches, while deciduous trees have a smaller number of offshoots along a branch but a greater height.

5. Sample answer: Deciduous trees live in temperate areas with a lot of sunlight and rainfall. Conifers live in colder, drier climates without as much sunlight.

6. Sample answer: Thin, waxy leaves collect less sunlight but help conifers from losing too much water; broad leaves that fall off in autumn take advantage of the larger amounts of sunlight in spring and summer but fall off to conserve scarce resources during the winter months.

7. Accept all reasonable answers. Responses should indicate that both kinds of trees need the same things (sunlight, nutrients, water, and so on) and that each group shows adaptations to certain types of environments.

8. Accept all reasonable answers.

QUICK LAB INDEPENDENT *Inquiry*

Homeostasis and Adaptations

In this lab, you will observe tree leaves and use what you know about biology to determine how the characteristics of a leaf relate to a plant's need to maintain homeostasis.

PROCEDURE

❶ Collect specimens of various deciduous and coniferous tree leaves from the vicinity of your school or, alternatively, select from a variety of tree leaves preselected by your teacher if fresh specimens are not readily available.

❷ Sketch each specimen in your journal and list their distinctive characteristics.

❸ Determine which leaves look similar and group them, listing the common characteristics of each group.

_____

_____

_____

_____

_____

❹ Extend your list from Step 3 to include the characteristics of the trees that the leaves came from. Do you notice any similarities between them?

_____

_____

_____

_____

_____

OBJECTIVES

• Define homeostasis.

• Explain why homeostasis is important for an organism's survival.

• Explain how homeostasis is maintained at the level of an organism.

MATERIALS

For each group

• camera (optional)

• journal

• pencil or pen

Quick Lab continued

5 Using what you know about each category of tree, describe the climate conditions where they live.

_____

_____

_____

_____

_____

6 Compare the list of living conditions and common characteristics, or adaptations, for each category. Suggest ways that the characteristics you observed relate to the environment in which the trees live.

_____

_____

_____

_____

_____

7 Examine your suggestions for both trees and highlight areas where the two groups of trees responded to similar needs in different ways. What explains those differences?

_____

_____

_____

_____

_____

8 Animals have to cope with challenges too. Can you list adaptations some animals have that allow them to live with several of the environmental challenges you listed for trees?

_____

_____

_____

_____

_____

EXPLORATION LAB DIRECTED *Inquiry* AND GUIDED *Inquiry*

Diffusion GENERAL

👥 Small Groups
🕐 45 minutes

LAB RATINGS

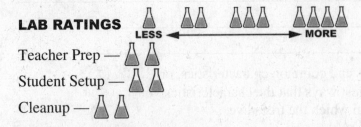

Teacher Prep —
Student Setup —
Cleanup —

SAFETY INFORMATION

Remind students to review all safety cautions and icons before beginning this lab. Students should exercise caution when working with or moving glass jars; additionally, students should work with gloves and goggles on because iodine has the ability to leave heavy stains. Instruct students to keep the test tube of Lugol's iodine in the beaker to prevent it from tipping over. Warn students not to try to clean up any iodine that spills when they pour it into the pouch; rather, they should inform you of any spill. Instruct students to wash and dry their hands after completing this activity.

TEACHER NOTES

In this activity, students will discover how diffusion is affected by environmental conditions and how diffusion relates to homeostasis by observing the interaction between a cornstarch solution and an iodine solution separated by a plastic membrane. Lugol's iodine causes cornstarch to turn a blue-black color. Provide each team with a test tube containing 10 mL of one of the three Lugol's iodine solutions (A, B, or C). Students will run several trials in which they vary the concentration of iodine in their setup. They will observe how the rate of diffusion of iodine across the plastic membrane varies with iodine concentration. Different groups will use solutions at different temperatures in order to investigate whether environmental conditions play a role as well.

   Prepare the cornstarch solution for each group by dissolving 1 tablespoon of cornstarch in 1 cup of water. Prepare the iodine solutions by mixing iodine with water in the quantities listed below. Each group should receive one of these solutions.

Solution	Iodine	Water
A	2 tsp	1 cup
B	1 tsp	1 cup
C	½ tsp	1 cup

MATERIALS

For each group
- cornstarch solution, cold
- cornstarch solution, warm
- cylinder, graduated
- jar, small
- plastic wrap
- rubber band
- scissors
- test tube containing 10 mL Lugol's iodine solution

For each student
- gloves
- lab apron
- safety goggles

My Notes

_____
_____
_____
_____
_____

Exploration Lab continued

Warn students to check their plastic wrap for tears, holes, or rips before they place it in the jar. Also have them make sure that the plastic wrap extends below the surface of the cornstarch solution before they pour in the iodine solution. This helps prevent stretching of the plastic that could lead to tears.

Tip Discuss the concept of energy as heat in relation to particle motion, a crucial concept because energy as heat in the fluid drives the diffusion process; however, let the students try to establish that connection first.

Student Tip Diffusion is a process dependent on the motion of molecules; what environmental factor directly affects that motion?

Skills Focus Making Hypotheses, Making Observations, Drawing Conclusions

MODIFICATION FOR INDEPENDENT Inquiry

Provide students with lab procedure and datasheets and introduce or review the concept of diffusion. Students will be told to investigate the effects of time and temperature on diffusion but they will be allowed to decide how to go about determining those effects and which groups will investigate which conditions.

Answer Key for DIRECTED Inquiry

FORM A HYPOTHESIS

1. Sample answer: The higher the concentration of iodine on one side of a membrane, the <u>greater</u> will be the amount of iodine that will move through the membrane because <u>particles tend to move until they are equal in concentration on both sides of the membrane</u>.

2. Sample answer: The higher the temperature, the <u>faster</u> will be the rate of iodine movement through the membrane because of an <u>increase</u> in particle motion.

FORM A PREDICTION

7. Accept all reasonable answers.
   Teacher Prompt Do you think the iodine will move? How?

MAKE OBSERVATIONS

10. Accept all reasonable answers.
11. Accept all reasonable answers.
12. Sample answers: jar size, amount of cornstarch, plastic wrap
13. Both temperature and iodine concentration are being used as independent variables.
14. The color of the cornstarch is the dependent variable because this is what we observe changing as iodine diffuses across the membrane.
15. Accept all reasonable answers. Drawings should have labels to show how iodine moved during the experiment.

ANALYZE THE RESULTS

16. Sample answer: The iodine moved through the plastic membrane into the cornstarch solution. I could tell because the color of the cornstarch solution changed.

17. Sample answer: The cornstarch solution contains larger molecules. They are too large to pass through holes in the membrane.

DRAW CONCLUSIONS

18. Solution A

19. Sample answer: Solution A appeared higher in concentration because it was darker in color than the others.

20. Answers will vary but students should demonstrate an understanding of the concept of diffusion.

21. Answers will vary but students should demonstrate an understanding that an increase in concentration results in greater diffusion of a substance from one side of a membrane to the other and that raising the temperature increases the rate of movement during diffusion.

Connect TO THE ESSENTIAL QUESTION

22. Accept all reasonable answers.

Answer Key for GUIDED Inquiry

FORM A HYPOTHESIS

1. Sample answer: The higher the concentration of iodine on one side of a membrane, the greater will be the amount of iodine that will move through the membrane because particles tend to move until they are equal in concentration on both sides of the membrane.

2. Sample answer: The higher the temperature, the faster will be the rate of iodine movement through the membrane because of an increase in particle motion.

FORM A PREDICTION

7. Accept all reasonable answers.
   Teacher Prompt Do you think the iodine will move? How?

MAKE OBSERVATIONS

10. Accept all reasonable answers.

11. Accept all reasonable answers.

12. Sample answers: jar size, amount of cornstarch, plastic wrap

13. Both temperature and iodine concentration are being used as independent variables.

14. The color of the cornstarch is the dependent variable because this is what we observe changing as iodine diffuses across the membrane.

15. Accept all reasonable answers. Drawings should have labels to show how iodine moved during the experiment.

Exploration Lab continued

ANALYZE THE RESULTS

16. Sample answer: The iodine moved through the plastic membrane into the cornstarch solution. I could tell because the color of the cornstarch solution changed.

17. Sample answer: The cornstarch solution contains larger molecules. They are too large to pass through holes in the membrane.

DRAW CONCLUSIONS

18. Solution A

19. Sample answer: Solution A appeared higher in concentration because it was darker in color than the others.

20. Answers will vary but the students should demonstrate an understanding of the concept of diffusion.

21. Answers will vary but students should demonstrate an understanding that an increase in concentration results in greater diffusion of a substance from one side of a membrane to the other and that raising the temperature increases the rate of movement during diffusion.

Connect TO THE ESSENTIAL QUESTION

22. Accept all reasonable answers.

EXPLORATION LAB DIRECTED *Inquiry*

Diffusion

Cells rely on diffusion as a means by which some materials pass in or out of the cell. The cell membrane forms a barrier between the inside of the cell and the external environment. It is across this membrane that some materials enter the cell and other materials exit the cell. Movement of materials by diffusion affects the cell's ability to maintain homeostasis.

In this lab, you will observe the process of diffusion. You will use iodine, cornstarch, and plastic wrap to model the process of diffusion. You will hypothesize what effects concentration and temperature have upon the diffusion process and then set up an experiment to test your hypotheses.

PROCEDURE

FORM A HYPOTHESIS

❶ Write a hypothesis to explain how concentration will affect the extent of diffusion of iodine through a membrane. Fill in the following blanks to form your hypothesis:

The higher the concentration of iodine on one side of a membrane, the _____ will be the amount of iodine that will move through the membrane because

_____.

FORM A HYPOTHESIS

❷ Write a hypothesis to explain how the temperature of the solution will affect the rate of diffusion of iodine through a membrane. Fill in the following blanks to form your hypothesis:

The higher the temperature, the _____ will be the rate of iodine movement through the membrane because of a(n) _____ in particle motion.

TEST THE HYPOTHESIS

❸ Fill a small jar about three-fourths full with the cornstarch solution. Half the groups will use the cold solution, and the other half will use the warm solution.

❹ Place the plastic wrap inside the jar so that the plastic is pushed down a little below the surface of the cornstarch solution, forming a pouch.

❺ Use a rubber band to secure the plastic wrap tightly around the mouth of the jar.

OBJECTIVE

- Investigate how concentration and temperature affect diffusion across a membrane.

MATERIALS

For each group
- cornstarch solution, cold
- cornstarch solution, warm
- cylinder, graduated
- jar, small
- plastic wrap
- rubber band
- scissors
- test tube containing 10 mL Lugol's iodine solution

For each student
- gloves
- lab apron
- safety goggles

Exploration Lab continued

6 Pour the iodine solution that you are given (A, B, or C) into the plastic wrap pouch. Carefully screw the lid onto the jar. Use scissors to trim the excess plastic wrap around the lid.

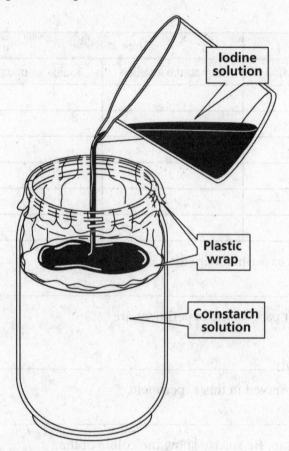

Iodine solution

Plastic wrap

Cornstarch solution

FORM A PREDICTION

7 Make a prediction about how the solution will change with the addition of the iodine.

_____

_____

MAKE OBSERVATIONS

8 Observe the color of the cornstarch solution and the color of the iodine solution and record your observations in Table 1.

9 Wait 20 minutes (min) and watch for color changes in your solutions.

10 After 20 min, examine the iodine solution inside the plastic membrane pouch. Use Table 1 to record any color changes you see.

Exploration Lab continued

11 Examine the cornstarch solution below the plastic membrane. Use Table 1 to record any color changes you see.

TABLE 1. COLOR CHANGES

Solution	Color at 0 min		Color at 20 min	
	Cornstarch solution	Iodine solution	Cornstarch solution	Iodine solution
A (cold)				
B (cold)				
C (cold)				
A (warm)				
B (warm)				
C (warm)				

12 Identify the constants. What parts of the experiment are the same for all groups?

_____

13 Identify the independent variables. What parts of the experiment are different for each group?

_____

14 Identify the dependent variable being observed in this experiment.

_____

15 Draw before and after pictures of the setup. Be sure to show the colors of the solutions on both sides of the membrane in each drawing. Also indicate the darkness of the colors. Use arrows to show the direction that the iodine or cornstarch solution moved through the plastic membrane.

ANALYZE THE RESULTS

16 **Analyzing Observations** Did cornstarch move through the plastic into the iodine, or did iodine move through the plastic into the cornstarch? How can you tell?

_____

_____

Exploration Lab continued

17 **Explaining Observations** Based on your observations, which solution contains larger molecules—cornstarch or iodine? Why weren't the larger molecules able to pass through the membrane?

_____

_____

DRAW CONCLUSIONS

18 **Evaluating Hypotheses** Which iodine solution (A, B, or C) produced the largest color change?

_____

_____

19 **Interpreting Results** Which solution had the highest concentration of iodine? How do you know?

_____

_____

_____

20 **Explaining Observations** What factors affect the movement of different substances through a membrane?

_____

_____

_____

21 **Applying Concepts** Did environmental conditions play a role in the results of this experiment?

_____

_____

_____

Connect **TO THE ESSENTIAL QUESTION**

22 **Applying Concepts** Name two real-life situations in which diffusion occurs.

_____

_____

_____

EXPLORATION LAB GUIDED *Inquiry*

Diffusion

Cells rely on diffusion as a means by which some materials pass in or out of the cell. The cell membrane forms a barrier between the inside of the cell and the external environment. It is across this membrane that some materials enter the cell and other materials exit the cell. Movement of materials by diffusion affects the cell's ability to maintain homeostasis.

    In this lab, you will observe the process of diffusion. You will use iodine, cornstarch, and plastic wrap to model the process of diffusion. You will hypothesize what effects concentration and temperature have upon the diffusion process and then set up an experiment to test your hypotheses.

PROCEDURE

FORM A HYPOTHESIS

❶ Write a hypothesis to explain how concentration will affect diffusion of material through a membrane.

_____

_____

FORM A HYPOTHESIS

❷ Write a hypothesis to explain how the temperature of the solution will affect diffusion of material through a membrane.

_____

_____

TEST THE HYPOTHESIS

❸ Fill a small jar about three-fourths full with the cornstarch solution. Half the groups will use the cold solution, and the other half will use the warm solution

❹ Place the plastic wrap inside the jar so that the plastic is pushed down a little below the surface of the cornstarch solution, forming a pouch.

❺ Use a rubber band to secure the plastic wrap tightly around the mouth of the jar.

OBJECTIVE

• Investigate how concentration and temperature affect diffusion across a membrane.

MATERIALS

For each group

• cornstarch solution, cold
• cornstarch solution, warm
• cylinder, graduated
• jar, small
• plastic wrap
• rubber band
• scissors
• test tube containing 10 mL Lugol's iodine solution

For each student

• gloves
• lab apron
• safety goggles

Exploration Lab continued

6 Pour the iodine solution that you are given (A, B, or C) into the plastic wrap pouch.

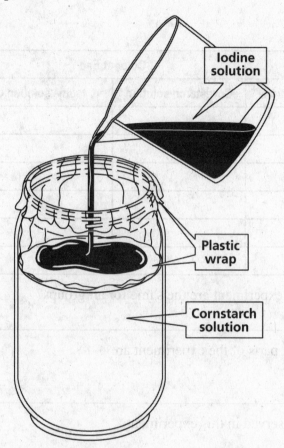

Iodine solution

Plastic wrap

Cornstarch solution

FORM A PREDICTION

7 Make a prediction about how the solution will change when the iodine is added.

_____

_____

MAKE OBSERVATIONS

8 Observe and record the color of the cornstarch solution and the color of the iodine solution.

9 As a team, set a time span (<30 minutes) to watch for color changes in your solutions.

10 After time has expired, examine the iodine solution inside the plastic membrane. Use Table 1 to record any color changes you see.

Exploration Lab continued

11 Examine the cornstarch solution outside the plastic membrane. Use Table 1 to record any color changes you see.

TABLE 1. COLOR CHANGES

Solution	Color at Start		Color at End	
	Cornstarch solution	Iodine solution	Cornstarch solution	Iodine solution
A (cold)				
B (cold)				
C (cold)				
A (warm)				
B (warm)				
C (warm)				

12 Identify the constants. What parts of the experiment are the same for all groups?

_____

13 Identify the independent variables. What parts of the experiment are different for each group?

_____

14 Identify the dependent variable being observed in this experiment.

_____

15 Draw before and after pictures of the setup on a separate sheet of paper. Be sure to show the colors of the solutions on both sides of the membrane in each drawing. Also indicate the darkness of the colors. Use arrows to show the direction that the iodine or cornstarch solution moved through the plastic membrane.

ANALYZE THE RESULTS

16 **Analyzing Observations** Did cornstarch move through the plastic into the iodine, or did iodine move through the plastic into the cornstarch? How can you tell?

_____

_____

17 **Explaining Observations** Based on your observations, which solution contains larger molecules—cornstarch or iodine? Why weren't the larger molecules able to pass through the membrane?

_____

_____

Exploration Lab continued

DRAW CONCLUSIONS

18 **Evaluating Hypotheses** Which iodine solution (A, B, or C) produced the largest color change?

_____

_____

19 **Interpreting Results** Which solution had the highest concentration of iodine? How do you know?

_____

_____

20 **Explaining Observations** What factors affect the movement of different substances through a membrane?

_____

_____

21 **Applying Concepts** Did environmental conditions play a role in the results of this experiment? Explain.

_____

_____

_____

Connect TO THE ESSENTIAL QUESTION

22 **Applying Concepts** Name two real-life situations in which diffusion occurs.

_____

_____

_____

QUICK LAB DIRECTED Inquiry

Plant Cell Structures GENERAL

👥 Student pairs
🕐 15 minutes

LAB RATINGS

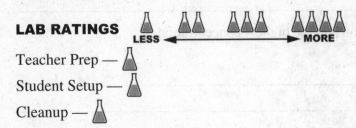

LESS ⬅————————➡ MORE

Teacher Prep —

Student Setup —

Cleanup —

MATERIALS

For each pair
- colored pencils, assorted
- microscope, compound
- prepared slides, unknown (2)

For each student
- paper, blank
- safety goggles

My Notes

_____

_____

_____

_____

_____

SAFETY INFORMATION

Remind students to review all safety cautions and icons before beginning this lab. Students should use caution when handling slides and microscopes, as broken glass can cause injuries. Advise students not to try to clean up broken glass themselves, but to report it instead. Warn students that a microscope's light source can cause eye damage if set too high.

TEACHER NOTES

In this activity, students will observe prepared slides to examine and compare the structures of different plant cells. If possible, provide students with one sample of a plant tissue containing many chloroplasts (e.g., an *Elodea* leaf) and one sample of a plant tissue containing few or no chloroplasts (e.g., an onion bulb). Cover any labels on prepared slides, and simply label slides "A" and "B." At the end of the exercise, you should provide students with the identities of their samples.

Tip This lab may help students understand how cell structures vary depending on function.

Student Tip Ask for help if you cannot get your specimen into focus.

Skills Focus Practicing Lab Techniques, Making Observations, Drawing Conclusions

MODIFICATION FOR GUIDED Inquiry

Provide students with the materials listed, and ask them to think about how examining cell structure can help determine the function of a cell or tissue. Encourage them to examine a variety of specimens and record or draw their observations. Ask students about their results, and encourage them to discuss their findings with the rest of the class. Have students brainstorm in groups what the functions of their tissue specimens might be. You may wish to eventually reveal the identities of the specimens and see how accurate the students' interpretations were.

Answer Key

4. Answers will vary.

5. Answers will vary.

6. Sample answer: Both cells have cell walls and nuclei, but one cell has several chloroplasts and the other does not seem to have any.

7. Sample answer: I think the first sample came from a leaf because it is green and has a lot of chloroplasts. The second sample probably came from a root or another structure that grows underground because it doesn't have chloroplasts and probably doesn't get much exposure to sunlight.

8. Sample answer: The *Elodea* leaf probably has a lot of chloroplasts because the leaves are the parts of the plant that capture the most sunlight and perform photosynthesis. The onion bulb does not have chloroplasts because it stays underground and stores energy. It does not create energy through photosynthesis.

Plant Cell Structures

In this lab, you will observe different samples of plant tissue using a microscope. You will examine cellular structures in each sample and explain how your observations relate to the function of each plant tissue.

PROCEDURE

❶ Place a **prepared slide** of plant tissue onto the **microscope**.

❷ Set the microscope on low power to examine the cells.

❸ Switch to high power and examine a single cell.

❹ On a separate piece of **paper**, draw one cell as it appears at high magnification. Try to identify and label as many structures as possible, including the cell wall, cell membrane, nucleus, cytoplasm, chloroplasts, mitochondria, and vacuoles.

❺ Repeat Steps 1–4 using the other prepared slide.

❻ How do the two cells you drew look alike? How do they differ?

_____

_____

_____

_____

_____

_____

_____

_____

_____

_____

_____

OBJECTIVES

- Compare cellular structures of different plant specimens.
- Relate cell structure to function.

MATERIALS

For each student pair

- colored pencils, assorted
- microscope, compound
- prepared slides, unknown (2)

For each student

- paper, blank
- safety goggles

Quick Lab continued

7 From what part of the plants' anatomy do you think each sample came?
Explain your answer.

_____

_____

_____

_____

_____

_____

_____

_____

_____

8 Ask your teacher for the identity of each of your samples. Explain how the
number of chloroplasts present in each sample could relate to the function of
the tissue.

_____

_____

_____

_____

_____

_____

_____

_____

_____

_____

_____

_____

_____

_____

QUICK LAB **DIRECTED** *Inquiry*

Investigate Carbon Dioxide GENERAL

👥 Student pairs
🕐 20 minutes

LAB RATINGS

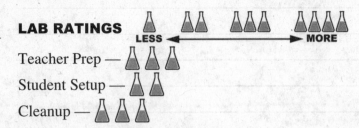

LESS ⟵⟶ MORE

Teacher Prep —

Student Setup —

Cleanup —

SAFETY INFORMATION

Remind students to review all safety cautions and icons before beginning this lab. Students should wear safety goggles during all portions of this experiment. They should not allow limewater to come into contact with skin. Any skin exposed should be rinsed immediately under running water. Students should not try to clean up spilled limewater but should be instructed to notify you of any spills as soon as they occur.

TEACHER NOTES

In this activity, students work in pairs to take three samples of air and test each sample for the presence of carbon dioxide. They use a plastic syringe to collect air samples and jars of limewater for the actual testing procedure.

Limewater is a saturated aqueous solution of calcium hydroxide. It can be made by adding a teaspoon of calcium hydroxide to 4 liters (L) of distilled water. With stirring, most of the calcium hydroxide will go into solution; however, not all will dissolve. This is expected because a saturated solution is one that contains the maximum amount of a solute dissolved in the solvent. To remove undissolved solute, pass this solution through a funnel lined with filter paper into a new container. Following the activity, limewater samples should be diluted with several volumes of water before they are disposed in the sink. Yeast samples may be discarded in the trash.

The bag with the yeast will be ready for air collection when it is slightly bubbled. The yeast will start to respire much more quickly if warm water is used and it is kept in a warm place.

Tip Have students set up the activity at the beginning of the class period. Then continue with the lesson while the yeast sample respires. Have students return to finish the lab in the last fifteen minutes of class.

Skills Focus Comparing Events, Explaining Results

MATERIALS

For each student pair
- bag, sealable plastic
- jars of limewater, 15 mL each (3 jars)
- spoon, plastic
- straw
- sugar, granulated
- syringe, small plastic
- yeast, active dry
- water, distilled

For each student
- gloves
- lab apron
- safety goggles

My Notes

_____

_____

_____

_____

_____

Quick Lab continued

MODIFICATION FOR GUIDED *Inquiry*

Do not provide students with a summary table for recording observations. Ask students to read through the procedure before starting the activity and to develop a table for recording their observations as they conduct their tests.

Answer Key

1. Accept all reasonable answers.

2. Students should note that the bag has inflated with gas.

3. Students should note that the limewater samples are all clear and colorless.

4. Students should observe that no change occurs in the limewater. Point out that the atmosphere contains carbon dioxide; however, the concentration of carbon dioxide in the atmosphere is too low to change the appearance of the limewater.

5. Students should observe that the air above the yeast culture causes the limewater to turn milky or cloudy.

6. Students should observe that their own exhaled air causes the limewater to turn milky or cloudy.

7. Sample results are shown:

SUMMARY OF OBSERVATIONS

	Limewater appearance before exposure to air sample	Limewater appearance after exposure to air sample
Air in classroom	Clear and colorless	Clear and colorless
Air from yeast culture	Clear and colorless	Cloudy, milky
Exhaled air from human	Clear and colorless	Cloudy, milky

8. Accept all reasonable answers. Look for students to recognize that both yeast and humans produce carbon dioxide as a waste product, which explains why the limewater turned cloudy in these two cases. Students should recognize that carbon dioxide results from cellular respiration.

9. Accept all reasonable answers. Look for students to recognize that yeast and humans are similar in that they both carry out cellular respiration and release carbon dioxide as a waste product of this process.

QUICK LAB DIRECTED *Inquiry*

Investigate Carbon Dioxide

All living organisms exchange matter, including gases, with their environment. Organisms need matter as a source of chemical building blocks for constructing cell parts. They also need matter as a source of chemical energy for fueling cellular reactions. As organisms use matter, they transform it. Some matter is retained by organisms and some is expelled as waste. In this activity, you will test air samples to observe one type of matter released by living organisms as waste.

PROCEDURE

1 With your partner, take a few minutes to set up a growing yeast culture. Do this by adding a spoonful of granulated sugar to 20 milliliters (mL) distilled water in a sealable plastic bag. Mix this until the sugar completely dissolves. Then add a spoonful of active dry yeast and seal the bag. Flatten the bag before sealing so as to remove as much air as possible. Use your hand to gently massage the bag. On the lines below, note your observations of the bag and the culture inside. Then allow the bag to sit undisturbed for 30 minutes (min) at room temperature.

_____

_____

_____

2 At the end of the 30 min incubation time, note your observations of the bag and the culture inside. Has any noticeable change occurred?

_____

_____

3 Obtain a plastic syringe and three jars of limewater from your teacher. All three limewater samples should be identical. Limewater is clear, but turns milky in the presence of carbon dioxide. Below, note your observations of these samples.

_____

_____

_____

OBJECTIVE

- Investigate the presence of carbon dioxide in various air samples.

MATERIALS

For each student pair
- bag, sealable plastic
- jars of limewater (saturated solution of calcium hydroxide) (15 mL each) (3 jars)
- spoon, plastic
- straw
- sugar, granulated
- syringe, small plastic
- yeast, active dry
- water, distilled

For each student
- gloves
- lab apron
- safety goggles

❹ Pull back on the plunger of the syringe. As you do, air will be drawn up inside the syringe. Have your partner open one of the jars of limewater. Without touching the liquid in the jar, carefully insert the syringe into the mouth of the jar and expel the air sample into the jar. Quickly remove the syringe, replace the jar lid, tighten the lid, and swirl the contents. Do you observe any changes in the limewater? Record your observations.

_____

_____

❺ Repeat Step 4 but use the syringe to sample the air inside the bag with your actively growing yeast culture. Expel this air into a second limewater jar, cap, and swirl. Do you observe any changes in this limewater sample? Record your observations.

_____

_____

❻ For your last trial, open the third jar of limewater; inhale through your nose and use the straw to exhale into the jar. Quickly cap and swirl as before. Do you observe any changes in this limewater sample? Record your observations.

_____

_____

❼ In the table below, summarize your observations.

SUMMARY OF OBSERVATIONS

	Limewater appearance before exposure to air sample	Limewater appearance after exposure to air sample
Air in classroom		
Air from yeast culture		
Exhaled air from human		

❽ Explain any differences in the limewater appearance after exposure to the three air samples. What cellular process accounts for these differences?

_____

_____

_____

❾ Did the results surprise you? What do these results say about any similarities or differences between yeast and humans?

_____

_____

_____

S.T.E.M. LAB GUIDED Inquiry AND INDEPENDENT Inquiry

Investigate Rate of Photosynthesis GENERAL

👥 Small Groups

🕐 One 45-minute class period and about 5 minutes per day for 5 days

LAB RATINGS

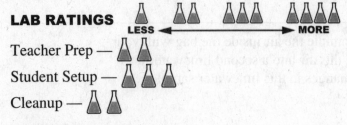

LESS ⬅️➡️ MORE

Teacher Prep —

Student Setup —

Cleanup —

SAFETY INFORMATION

Remind students to review all safety cautions and icons before beginning this lab. Inform students that spills are to be expected when they manipulate the funnel and test tube. However, caution students to use care when inverting the test tube in the baking soda solution to minimize any spills. Tell them to use paper towels to clean up any spills. Have students wash and dry their hands after completing this activity.

TEACHER NOTES

In this activity, students will decide on one variable to study to see whether it affects the amount of oxygen production in photosynthesizing *Elodea* plants. Students are provided with a basic procedure that they can use for setting up a system for measuring oxygen production by *Elodea*; however, they will choose the variable they will study and will make the final choices for design of their experiment to test their chosen variable.

The materials listed on the student page are enough for a pair or small group of students. *Elodea* (whose common name is waterweed) is a common aquarium plant and can be found at some pet stores and most places that sell aquarium fish. A 5% solution of baking soda and water can be made by adding water to 50 grams (g) of baking soda until the volume is 1 liter (L) and mixing. (You would add about 950 milliliters (mL) of water.) Students may find that the funnel has a tendency to float. To counteract this, have them place a large washer over the stem of the funnel to hold it down over the *Elodea* sprigs. Be sure that the funnel fits completely inside the beaker. Also be sure that students use the same mass of *Elodea* in each beaker if *Elodea* mass is not the variable being tested.

You may want to have students practice placing the test tube over the inverted funnel using water before students do so with the baking soda solution. It may take two or three tries to get the test tube over the funnel stem without letting any air into the tube. Tell the students the following: "First, fill the test tube with the solution. Place your thumb tightly over the opening so that air cannot get in. Submerge your thumb and the top of the test tube. Once the top of the test tube is underwater, you can remove your thumb from the opening of the test tube and maneuver the test tube over the stem of the funnel. Be sure that you have the *Elodea* in place under the funnel before you begin!"

MATERIALS

For the class
• balance

For each group
• baking soda-and-water solution, 5% (1 L)
• beaker (600 mL) (2)
• *Elodea* sprigs, 20 cm long (2-3)
• funnels, (2)
• ruler, metric
• test tubes (2)

For each student
• lab apron
• safety goggles

My Notes

_____

_____

_____

_____

_____

S.T.E.M. Lab continued

Tip It will be very difficult for students to test the effect of temperature differences on oxygen production and so this variable is one that is not recommended for students to test.

Skills Focus Designing Experiments, Graphing Data, Comparing Results

MODIFICATION FOR DIRECTED Inquiry

Assign each student group the variable they will study and assist them with their experimental design. Provide students with the data table you would like them to use. During the analysis portion of the lab, instruct students to plot the amount of gas produced in millimeters on the *y*-axis versus day on the *x*-axis of their graph.

Answer Key for GUIDED Inquiry

ASK A QUESTION

1. Accept all reasonable answers.

FORM A HYPOTHESIS

2. Accept all reasonable answers.

DEVELOP A PLAN

4. Accept all reasonable answers.

MAKE OBSERVATIONS

6. Check data to be sure students measured gas levels properly and made correct calculations of the amounts of gas produced each day.

ANALYZE THE RESULTS

7. Check graphs to be sure students correctly plotted their data and that control and experimental data points are clearly differentiated by color or by symbol.

8. Answers will vary. Be sure students are correctly describing the data they obtained.

DRAW CONCLUSIONS

9. Answers will vary. Be sure students are correctly describing the data they obtained.

10. Answers will vary. Be sure students discuss actual difficulties they encountered in their experiment.

Connect TO THE ESSENTIAL QUESTION

11. Answers will vary. Students should relate their experimental results to facts about photosynthesis.

Answer Key for INDEPENDENT Inquiry

ASK A QUESTION

1. Accept all reasonable answers.

FORM A HYPOTHESIS

2. Accept all reasonable answers.

DEVELOP A PLAN

4. Accept all reasonable answers.

MAKE OBSERVATIONS

6. Check data tables for completeness and general design. Check data to be sure students measured gas levels properly and made correct calculations of the amounts of gas produced each day. An example data table is shown:

AMOUNT OF GAS PRESENT IN CONTROL AND EXPERIMENTAL TEST TUBES

| Days of exposure to light | Control test tube | | Experimental test tube | |
	Total amount of gas present (mm)	Amount of gas produced per day (mm)	Total amount of gas present (mm)	Amount of gas produced per day (mm)
0				
1				
2				
3				
4				
5				

ANALYZE THE RESULTS

7. Check graphs to be sure students correctly plotted their data and that control and experimental data points are clearly differentiated by color or by symbol.

8. Answers will vary. Be sure students are correctly describing the data they obtained.

DRAW CONCLUSIONS

9. Answers will vary. Be sure students are correctly describing the data they obtained.

10. Answers will vary. Be sure students discuss actual difficulties they encountered in their experiment.

Connect TO THE ESSENTIAL QUESTION

11. Answers will vary. Students should relate their experimental results to facts about photosynthesis.

S.T.E.M. LAB GUIDED *Inquiry*

Investigate Rate of Photosynthesis

Plants use photosynthesis to make food. Photosynthesis produces oxygen gas. Humans and many other organisms cannot live without this oxygen. Oxygen is necessary for cellular respiration. In this activity, you will measure the oxygen produced by an aquatic plant known as *Elodea*.

    Your group will measure oxygen production over a five-day period and compare the amount of oxygen produced when you change one variable. The number of plants you use depends on the design of your experiment. You need at least one control plant and one experimental plant. You may choose one of the following variables to explore: amount of light exposure, amount of available carbon dioxide, mass of *Elodea*, or another variable of your choice. You will then set up your experiment, collect data, and finally compare the amounts of gas produced in the control and experimental samples.

PROCEDURE

ASK A QUESTION

❶ Work within your group to decide what variable you would like to investigate. Write a question below in terms of the variable you will investigate in this lab. For example, if you were going to investigate the effect of temperature on the amount of oxygen production during photosynthesis in *Elodea*, your question might be framed: In *Elodea*, how does the amount of oxygen produced during photosynthesis at 22 °C compare with the amount produced at 35 °C?

_____

_____

_____

OBJECTIVE

• Compare the amount of gas produced by a photosynthesizing plant as a single variable is changed.

MATERIALS

For the class
• balance

For each group
• baking soda-and-water solution, 5% (1 L)
• beaker (600 mL) (2)
• *Elodea* sprigs, 20 cm long (2-3)
• funnels, (2)
• ruler, metric
• test tubes (2)

For each student
• lab apron
• safety goggles

FORM A HYPOTHESIS

2 Think about the question you will be trying to answer. Write a hypothesis that your experiment will test based on this question. Your hypothesis statement should be written in the following form: "The amount of oxygen produced will _____ when _____is _____ because _____." For example, "The amount of oxygen produced will increase when temperature is raised because photosynthetic reaction rates will increase in the plant cells." Write your hypothesis below.

_____

_____

DEVELOP A PLAN

3 Read through the general procedure for carrying out an example of a control for this experiment.

General Procedure for Measuring Oxygen Production in Photosynthesizing *Elodea*

a) Add 450 milliliters (mL) of baking soda-and-water solution to a beaker.

b) Put two or three sprigs of *Elodea* in the beaker. The baking soda will provide the *Elodea* with the carbon dioxide it needs for photosynthesis.

c) Place the wide end of the funnel over the *Elodea*. The small end of the funnel should be pointing up. The *Elodea* and the funnel should be completely under the solution.

d) Fill a test tube with the remaining baking soda-and-water solution. Place your thumb over the end of the test tube, and turn the test tube upside down. Make sure no air enters the test tube. Hold the opening of the test tube under the solution. Place the test tube over the small end of the funnel. Try not to let any solution out of the test tube.

e) Place the beaker setup in a well-lit area.

f) Record your data. If no air entered the test tube, record that there was 0 millimeters (mm) of gas in the test tube on day 0. If air got into the tube while you were placing it, measure the height of the column of air in the test tube in millimeters. Measure the gas in the test tube from the middle of the curve on the bottom of the upside-down test tube to the level of the solution. Record this number for day 0.

g) As described in the previous step, measure the amount of gas in the test tube each day for the next 5 days. Record your measurements in the appropriate column of your data table.

S.T.E.M. Lab continued

4 Discuss a plan for setting up control and experimental apparatuses to ensure a workable design for testing the hypothesis you posed in Step 2. Explain your plan below. Be sure to explain how the control will differ from the experimental setup and why that should allow you to obtain the data you need to test the hypothesis you posed. Obtain your teacher's approval for your plan.

_____

_____

_____

_____

_____

_____

TEST THE HYPOTHESIS

5 Set up your experiment according to your plan.

MAKE OBSERVATIONS

6 Use the following table for recording data. Proceed with data collection. Each day, calculate the amount of gas produced in each test tube. Subtract the amount of gas present on the previous day from the amount of gas present on the current day. Record these amounts in the third and fifth columns of your data table.

AMOUNT OF GAS PRESENT IN CONTROL AND EXPERIMENTAL TEST TUBES

Days of exposure to light	Control test tube		Experimental test tube	
	Total amount of gas present (mm)	Amount of gas produced per day (mm)	Total amount of gas present (mm)	Amount of gas produced per day (mm)
0				
1				
2				
3				
4				
5				

ANALYZE THE RESULTS

7 **Constructing Graphs** Make one graph to show your results. Include both your control and experimental results on the same graph. Use different colors or symbols to clearly distinguish the two sets of results.

S.T.E.M. Lab continued

8 **Describing Events** Based on your graph, how did the amount of gas produced change over time in the control and in the experimental samples?

_____

_____

_____

DRAW CONCLUSIONS

9 **Comparing Results** Do your results support your hypothesis? Explain.

_____

_____

_____

10 **Evaluating Experimental Design** What aspects of your experimental design worked well? What did not work well? Explain what you could have done differently that would have improved your ability to draw conclusions from your experiment.

_____

_____

_____

_____

Connect TO THE ESSENTIAL QUESTION

11 **Applying Concepts** How do your experimental findings support what you know about photosynthesis as the process plants use to obtain energy from the environment?

_____

_____

_____

Investigate Rate of Photosynthesis

Plants use photosynthesis to make food. Photosynthesis produces oxygen gas. Humans and many other organisms cannot live without this oxygen. Oxygen is necessary for cellular respiration. In this activity, you will measure the oxygen produced by an aquatic plant known as *Elodea*.

Your group will measure oxygen production over a five-day period and compare the amount of oxygen produced when you change one variable. The number of plants you use depends on the design of your experiment. You need at least one control plant and one experimental plant. You may choose one of the following variables to explore: amount of light exposure, amount of available carbon dioxide, mass of *Elodea*, or another variable of your choice. You will then set up your experiment, collect data, and finally compare the amounts of gas produced in the control and experimental samples.

PROCEDURE

ASK A QUESTION

1 Work within your group to decide what variable you would like to investigate. Write a question below in terms of the variable you will investigate in this lab. For example, if you decided to investigate the effect of temperature on the amount of oxygen produced during photosynthesis in *Elodea*, your question might be framed: In *Elodea*, how does the amount of oxygen produced during photosynthesis at 22 °C compare with the amount produced at 35 °C?

_____

_____

OBJECTIVE

• Compare the amount of gas produced by a photosynthesizing plant as a single variable is changed.

MATERIALS

For the class
• balance

For each group
• baking soda-and-water solution, 5% (1 L)
• beaker (600 mL) (2)
• *Elodea* sprigs, 20 cm long (2-3)
• funnels, (2)
• ruler, metric
• test tubes (2)

For each student
• lab apron
• safety goggles

S.T.E.M. Lab continued

FORM A HYPOTHESIS

❷ Think about the question you will be trying to answer. Write a hypothesis based on this question that your experiment will test. Your hypothesis statement should be written in the form, "The amount of oxygen produced will _____ when _____is _____ because _____." For example, "The amount of oxygen produced will increase when temperature is raised because photosynthetic reaction rates will increase in the plant cells." Write your hypothesis below.

_____

_____

DEVELOP A PLAN

❸ Read through the general procedure for carrying out an example of a control for this experiment.

General Procedure for Measuring Oxygen Production in Photosynthesizing *Elodea*

a) Add 450 milliliters (mL) of baking soda-and-water solution to a beaker.

b) Put two or three sprigs of *Elodea* in the beaker. The baking soda will provide the *Elodea* with the carbon dioxide it needs for photosynthesis.

c) Place the wide end of the funnel over the *Elodea*. The small end of the funnel should be pointing up. The *Elodea* and the funnel should be completely under the solution.

d) Fill a test tube with the remaining baking soda-and-water solution. Place your thumb over the end of the test tube, and turn the test tube upside down. Make sure no air enters the test tube. Hold the opening of the test tube under the solution. Place the test tube over the small end of the funnel. Try not to let any solution out of the test tube.

e) Place the beaker setup in a well-lit area.

f) Record your data. If no air entered the test tube, record that there was 0 millimeters (mm) of gas in the test tube on day 0. If air got into the tube while you were placing it, measure the height of the column of air in the test tube in millimeters. Measure the gas in the test tube from the middle of the curve on the bottom of the upside-down test tube to the level of the solution. Record this number for day 0.

g) As described in the previous step, measure the amount of gas in the test tube each day for the next 5 days. Record your measurements in the appropriate column of your data table.

S.T.E.M. Lab continued

4 Discuss a plan for setting up control and experimental apparatuses to ensure a workable design for testing the hypothesis you posed in Step 2. Explain your plan below. Be sure to explain how the control will differ from the experimental setup and why that should allow you to obtain the data you need to test the hypothesis you posed. Obtain your teacher's approval for your plan.

_____

_____

_____

_____

_____

TEST THE HYPOTHESIS

5 Set up your experiment according to your plan.

MAKE OBSERVATIONS

6 Develop a table for recording data. Show your data table in the space below and proceed with data collection.

ANALYZE THE RESULTS

7 **Constructing Graphs** Make one graph to show your results. Include both your control and experimental results on the same graph. Use different colors or symbols to clearly distinguish the two sets of results.

8 **Describing Events** Based on your graph, how did the amount of gas produced change over time in the control and in the experimental samples?

_____

_____

_____

S.T.E.M. Lab continued

DRAW CONCLUSIONS

9 **Comparing Results** Do your results support your hypothesis? Explain.

_____

_____

10 **Evaluating Experimental Design** What aspects of your experimental design worked well? What did not work well? Explain what you could have done differently that would have improved your ability to draw conclusions from your experiment.

_____

_____

_____

_____

Connect TO THE ESSENTIAL QUESTION

11 **Applying Concepts** How do your experimental findings support what you know about photosynthesis as the process plants use to obtain energy from the environment?

_____

_____

_____

_____

Modeling Mitosis GENERAL

👥 Small groups
🕐 30 minutes

LAB RATINGS

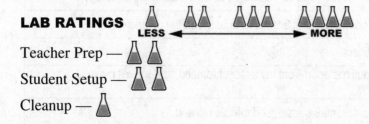

LESS ← → MORE

Teacher Prep —

Student Setup —

Cleanup —

TEACHER NOTES

In this lab, students model the phases of mitosis using physical movement. Encourage each group to have a "narrator" who describes the processes during each phase. If possible, have a student "documenter" who takes photos or video of the activity. Students can use this documentation to reinforce understanding.

Skills Focus Making Models, Applying Concepts

MODIFICATION FOR GUIDED *Inquiry*

Provide students with materials, and challenge them to model mitosis. You may permit them to use additional materials. If groups have difficulty getting started, encourage them to think about which cell features must be included and which can be omitted.

MATERIALS

For each group
• adhesive tape
• index cards
• markers
• materials for modeling cell structures involved in mitosis
• paper, optional
• self-stick notes

My Notes

_____

_____

_____

_____

_____

Answer Key

2. Sample answer:

Mitosis Phase	My Activity
Interphase	I form from the chromatin. Then I will be duplicated to form a sister chromosome.
Prophase	I wait for centrioles to form. Spindle fibers will form between the centrioles.
Metaphase	I attach to the spindle fibers.
Anaphase	The spindle fibers will pull me apart from my sister chromatid, and we will move to opposite ends of the cell.
Telophase	I will become part of the chromatin again, and mitosis will end.

4. Sample answer: I played the role of a chromosome. I was duplicated so that the genetic material in the parent and daughter cells was identical.

5. Sample answer: Errors are most likely to occur during interphase. I would model this by giving some chromatids colored stickers to indicate that they have an error.

6. Sample answer: Our demonstration did not show how the cell membrane changes during mitosis. We could use a large circle of string to model the cell membrane. The string could be moved to show how the cell membrane changes during mitosis.

QUICK LAB INDEPENDENT *Inquiry*

Modeling Mitosis

In this lab, you will model the phases of mitosis.

PROCEDURE

① As a team, review the phases of mitosis. On a piece of **paper**, list the cell structures and organelles involved in the process of mitosis. Then, decide how your team will demonstrate the process of mitosis for your class. Have each team member choose a role to play.

② Use the table below to plan your activity during each phase of mitosis. Make sure that you coordinate your activities as a team.

Mitosis Phase	My Activity
Interphase	
Prophase	
Metaphase	
Anaphase	
Telophase	

③ Use the **index cards** or **self-stick notes** to create a label that indicates the role you are playing. Use **tape** to attach the label to yourself where it can be clearly seen during your demonstration.

④ Which role did you play during the demonstration? How did you help to produce a cell that was identical to the original?

_____

_____

_____

_____

OBJECTIVES

- Identify the roles of cell structures and organelles during the process of mitosis.
- Describe the process of mitosis, and model how mitosis results in the production of a cell identical to the original.

MATERIALS

For each group
- adhesive tape
- index cards (10–15)
- markers
- materials for modeling cell structures involved in mitosis
- paper, optional
- self-stick notes

Quick Lab continued

5 During which phase of mitosis are genetic errors most likely to occur? How would you model this in your activity?

_____

_____

_____

_____

_____

_____

_____

_____

_____

6 How could you improve your demonstration to more accurately represent the process of mitosis?

_____

_____

_____

_____

_____

_____

_____

_____

_____

QUICK LAB GUIDED Inquiry

Mitosis Flipbooks GENERAL

👥 Small groups
🕐 30 minutes

LAB RATINGS

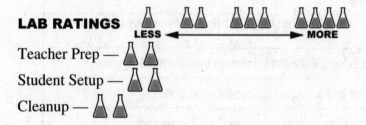

LESS ⟵————————⟶ MORE

Teacher Prep —
Student Setup —
Cleanup —

SAFETY INFORMATION

Remind students to review all safety cautions and icons before beginning this lab.

TEACHER NOTES

In this lab, students will be creating flipbooks that animate the process of mitosis. Strictly speaking, interphase is the stage of the cell cycle that precedes mitosis, but it is included in this activity to help students remember the importance of chromosome duplication prior to mitosis. This activity works best if the flipbooks are created from heavy stock paper. Also, you can greatly reduce the time required for students to prepare their flipbooks by creating and photocopying a simple empty cell template for each phase. You should be able to place at least eight empty cells on a letter-sized sheet of paper. Students can draw cell details in each blank cell and then cut out the cells to make the pages of the flipbook. This activity works best if students form teams of five so that each student can illustrate one phase of mitosis, plus interphase.

Skills Focus Making Models, Evaluating Methods

MODIFICATION FOR INDEPENDENT Inquiry

Challenge students to develop their own method to animate the process of mitosis. For example, students could use computer presentation software, a video camera, or a series of digital photographs in a slide show. If students use digital media to create their animation, encourage them to include voiceover narration that describes each phase of mitosis, plus interphase.

MATERIALS

For each group

- binder clips (2)
- blank index cards or templates containing empty cells
- markers
- paper
- scissors

My Notes

_____

_____

_____

_____

_____

Answer Key

2. Sample answer:

Phase	Description
Interphase	The chromosomes are duplicated.
Prophase	The centrioles form and move to opposite ends of the cell. Spindle fibers form between the centrioles.
Metaphase	The chromosome pairs attach to the spindle fibers and align between the centrioles.
Anaphase	The chromosome pairs separate and are pulled to opposite ends of the cell.
Telophase	The chromosomes are surrounded by nuclear membranes and mitosis ends.

4. Sample answer: I would add many more images so that the flipbook would take 80 minutes to flip through. Interphase would be the longest section, and anaphase would be the shortest section.

5. Sample answer: I would alter the flipbook so that it more accurately portrays the relative sizes of cell structures and organelles.

QUICK LAB GUIDED Inquiry

Mitosis Flipbooks

In this lab, you will work as a team to make a flipbook that animates the phases of mitosis, plus interphase.

PROCEDURE

1 Before you begin, work as a team to describe the events that occur during interphase and each phase of mitosis. Record your ideas in the table below.

Phase	Description
Interphase	
Prophase	
Metaphase	
Anaphase	
Telophase	

OBJECTIVES

- Identify how a cell changes during each phase of mitosis.
- Compare the process of mitosis with a model or simulation of mitosis.

MATERIALS

For each group
- binder clips (2)
- blank index cards or templates containing empty cells
- markers
- paper
- scissors

Quick Lab continued

❷ You will receive **materials** to create your flipbook. As a team, decide which phase of mitosis each team member will illustrate. Each team member should make a few practice illustrations so that the images in the flipbook appear similar.

❸ When the illustrations are complete, cut out the images so that each is a separate page. Order the pages in the correct sequence to represent the process of mitosis. Use the **binder clips** to secure one edge of the stack of pages to form a book. When you slowly flip the pages, you should see an animation of mitosis.

❹ Mitosis takes about 80 minutes to occur in onion cells. How would you alter your flipbook model to represent more accurately that span of time? Which section of the flipbook would be longest? Which section would be shortest?

_____

_____

_____

_____

_____

_____

_____

_____

❺ How could you alter your flipbook to more accurately represent the process of mitosis?

_____

_____

_____

_____

_____

_____

_____

_____

_____

QUICK LAB DIRECTED Inquiry

DNA, Chromosomes, and Cell Division GENERAL

👥 Student Pairs

🕐 15 minutes

LAB RATINGS

LESS ◄─────────► MORE

Teacher Prep —

Student Setup —

Cleanup —

MATERIALS
For each student pair
• bags, plastic, quart size (2)
• envelopes, standard (2)
• index cards, 3 × 5 (12)
• marker
• tape, transparent

SAFETY INFORMATION

Remind students to review all safety cautions and icons before beginning this lab.

My Notes
_____
_____
_____
_____
_____

TEACHER NOTES

In this activity students will make a model of a cell that focuses on the chromosomal nature of the cell's genetic information. Students will be given a limited set of materials to construct their model. They are asked to think of a way to use the materials to show the cell membrane, the cell nucleus, and the cell's DNA. They will use a code to indicate a unique trait of their choice for their cell on the DNA and then place the DNA in the cell nucleus, which is then placed inside the cell membrane. Groups exchange cells and then put their traded cells through cell division. As students take charge of the cell division, they also decode the DNA to learn what interesting trait their traded cell has.

Tip This activity may help students understand that DNA is a long molecule, that it carries genetic information, and that it is packaged in chromosomes.

Student Tip When stretched out, a DNA molecule is 300,000 times longer than the width of a typical cell nucleus.

Skills Focus Developing a Model, Applying Concepts

MODIFICATION FOR INDEPENDENT Inquiry

Provide students with the materials in this lab. Allow them to use the materials to develop their own model to explain the relationship between a DNA molecule and a chromosome.

Answer Key

2. Accept all reasonable answers. It is expected that students will use the plastic bag as the cell membrane, the envelope as the cell nucleus, and several index cards taped together in a linear sequence to represent the DNA.

3. Sample answer: The index cards (DNA) have to be folded like an accordion so that they will fit into the envelope (cell nucleus).

4. The folded-up DNA represents a chromosome.

5. Sample answer: We will take the DNA out of the nucleus to unfold it and copy it on new index cards that we tape together

   Teacher Prompt What happens to the chromatin in the early stages of cell division before the cell is divided? The chromatin is compacted into visible structures called chromosomes. The duplicated chromosomes remain in the nucleus until the nuclear membrane breaks down. Then we will put each copy into its own envelope and then into its own plastic bag. In the end we will have two cells, each with a copy of the DNA in its nucleus.

6. Sample answer: We have two cells and they are identical to each other.

7. Answers will vary depending on the coded information on the index cards.

8. Sample answer: In the model, the DNA had to be folded in order to fit into the nucleus. In a real cell, the same type of thing happens, too. The DNA is packaged into chromosomes that are much shorter in length than the DNA molecule when it is allowed to stretch out to its full length.

QUICK LAB DIRECTED Inquiry

DNA, Chromosomes, and Cell Division

DNA molecules are long molecules. They are about 300,000 times longer than the width of the cell nucleus! Each DNA molecule is wrapped and twisted around protein molecules forming chromatin. In the early stage of cell division, chromatin is compacted into chromosomes. At certain stages of the cell cycle, the chromosomes are visible as condensed structures. At other stages, they are not visible because they are more stretched out and not condensed. In this lab you will investigate the relationship between DNA and chromosomes using models.

PROCEDURE

❶ As a class, decide on a method for encoding the English alphabet. For example, assign numbers to letters starting with A=1, B=2, C=3, and so on. You will use this code to transmit information about the cell you design in the next step.

❷ With your partner, make a model of a cell that uses materials provided for you. Your cell must have a cell membrane, a nucleus, and a DNA molecule that when stretched out, is several times longer than the cell nucleus is wide. Your DNA molecule must contain information encoded on it that specifies one interesting trait of your cell. Brainstorm with your partner to think of a way to use the materials you have to make your cell model. Use your imagination to decide on a unique trait for your cell that you can encode in its DNA. Summarize your plan below for how you will make your cell model.

_____

_____

_____

_____

❸ Now make your cell model. What did you have to do to make your DNA molecule fit into the cell nucleus?

_____

_____

OBJECTIVES

- Create a model to show how cell division results in two new cells that have a full set of genetic material identical to the parent cell.
- Recognize that DNA is packaged into structures called chromosomes.

MATERIALS

For each student pair
- bags, plastic, quart size (2)
- envelopes, standard (2)
- index cards, 3 × 5 (12)
- marker
- tape, transparent

Quick Lab continued

4 What does the folded-up DNA represent?

_____

5 Now exchange your cell model with that from another group. The cell you just received is ready to undergo cell division. Assuming that you are in charge of making sure that it divides properly, what will you do to carry out cell division?

_____

_____

_____

_____

6 Use your materials to carry out the cell division process for the cell. How many cells do you have at the conclusion of your cell division process? How do they compare with each other?

_____

_____

_____

7 What unique trait does your cell have?

_____

_____

8 How is the packaging of DNA in your model similar to the packaging of DNA in a real cell nucleus?

_____

_____

_____

_____

EXPLORATION LAB GUIDED *Inquiry* **AND** INDEPENDENT *Inquiry*

Stages of the Cell Cycle GENERAL

👥 Student pairs

🕐 45 minutes

LAB RATINGS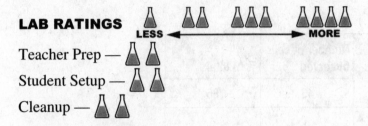

Teacher Prep —

Student Setup —

Cleanup —

MATERIALS

For each student pair
- microscope
- microscope slide, prepared onion root tip
- paper, graphing

For each student
- safety goggles

My Notes

_____

_____

_____

_____

_____

SAFETY INFORMATION

Remind students to review all safety cautions and icons before beginning this lab. Explain to students that broken glass (slides) should go in the designated container.

TEACHER NOTES

In this lab, students will examine a prepared slide of actively dividing cells in onion root tip. They will search the slide to find cells that represent different stages of the cell cycle and then count the number of cells at each stage within a randomly selected group of cells. Students can use these counts to draw conclusions about the length of time any one cell spends in each stage. A circle graph can be drawn to help students visualize how the cell cycle is organized in sequence and in time.

   If you do not have prepared slides, you can use the inner transparent skin of the onion, place it on a slide, add a drop of water and a drop of the iodine to stain the nuclei, and place a cover slip over it making sure no air bubbles are trapped during the cover slip placement.

Tip Remind the students to use caution when changing objectives on their microscope so that they don't accidentally break the prepared slide.

Skills Focus Analyzing Data, Making Graphs, Drawing Conclusions

MODIFICATION FOR DIRECTED *Inquiry*

Students should be directed at each point in the guided inquiry procedure so they have clear instructions about how to proceed to the next step. You may wish to allow students independence in choosing the type of graph that they draw, however. Be sure to have them explain their justification for the type of graph they choose.

Exploration Lab continued

Answer Key for GUIDED Inquiry

MAKE OBSERVATIONS

3. Sample answer: interphase, prophase, metaphase, anaphase, telophase, cytokinesis.

4. Accept all reasonable answers.

5. Sample data table.

	Stage of cell division	Number of cells observed	% of total
Mitosis	interphase	43	86
	prophase	3	6
	metaphase	1	2
	anaphase	1	2
	telophase and cytokinesis	1	4

ANALYZE THE RESULTS

6. Accept all reasonable answers. Students should demonstrate that they recognize a stage may be so short that it is not captured in their representative group of cells.

7. A circle graph will provide the best visual representation of the relative times spent at each stage because each section of the circle represents a category of the data. The entire circle represents all of the data. However, accept all answers from students who have supplied reasonable justification for their choice.

8. Check graphs to be sure that students graphed their own data accurately.

DRAW CONCLUSIONS

9. Answers will vary because the distribution of some stages within randomly selected groups of 50–60 cells may vary. However, interphase is the longest of the phases of the cell cycle. Be sure that students analyze their own data.

Connect TO THE ESSENTIAL QUESTION

10. Sample answer: The cell must have an organized way to copy its DNA and then divide its cell contents to allow the formation of two complete daughter cells. Having a specific sequence allows each daughter cell to receive the correct genetic information it needs.

Exploration Lab continued

Answer Key for INDEPENDENT Inquiry

DEVELOP A PLAN

2. Accept all reasonable answers.

Teacher Prompt How could you use the cells on a single slide to help you compare the time each stage takes?

MAKE OBSERVATIONS

3. Sample data table

Stage of cell division		Number of cells observed	% of total
	interphase	43	86
Mitosis	prophase	3	6
	metaphase	1	2
	anaphase	1	2
	telophase and cytokinesis	1	4

ANALYZE THE RESULTS

4. Accept all reasonable answers. Students should demonstrate that they recognize a stage may be so short that it is not captured in their representative group of cells.

5. A circle graph will provide the best visual representation of the relative times spent at each stage because each section of the circle represents a category of the data. The entire circle represents all of the data. However, accept all answers from students who have supplied reasonable justification for their choice.

6. Check graphs to be sure that students graphed their own data accurately.

DRAW CONCLUSIONS

7. Answers will vary because the distribution of some stages within randomly selected groups of cells may vary. However, interphase is the longest of the phases of the cell cycle. Be sure that students analyze their own data.

Connect TO THE ESSENTIAL QUESTION

8. Sample answer: The cell must have an organized way to copy its DNA and then divide its cell contents to allow the formation of two complete daughter cells. Having a specific sequence allows each daughter cell to receive the correct genetic information it needs.

EXPLORATION LAB GUIDED *Inquiry*

The Stages of the Cell Cycle

A cell passes through specific stages as it divides to form two daughter cells. Taken together, these stages make up the cell cycle. These events are considered cyclic because each generation of cells passes through the same cell cycle as the previous generation.

Each stage requires a different amount of time to complete. If you were to take a snapshot of a group of actively dividing cells, you would find a representative distribution of cells in each stage of the cell cycle. The number of cells you see in each stage gives an indication of how long a period of time the cell spends at that stage. For example, you would find very few cells at a stage that takes a very short time to complete, while you would find a large number of cells at a stage that takes a very long time to complete.

In this lab you will observe a stained microscope slide of actively dividing cells from an onion root tip. You will identify cells in each stage of the cell cycle and count the total number of cells you find at each stage. You can then construct a graph to show this distribution of cells across the stages of the cell cycle and draw conclusions about how long each stage takes to complete.

PROCEDURE

ASK A QUESTION

❶ In this lab, you will investigate the following question: How much time does a cell spend in each stage of the cell cycle?

MAKE OBSERVATIONS

❷ Adjust your microscope objective to the lowest power. Place a prepared onion root tip slide on the stage and move it around until you see the area just above the root tip. The cells in this area were actively dividing when the slide was made.

OBJECTIVES

- Identify the stages of the cell cycle from observations of a stained sample of onion root tip tissue.
- Count the number of cells representing each stage and use the data to draw conclusions about the length of time a cell spends in each stage.

MATERIALS

For each student pair
- microscope
- microscope slide
- paper, graphing
- prepared onion root tip tissue

For each student
- safety goggles

Exploration Lab continued

3 With your partner, discuss the various stages of the cell cycle that you will be identifying as you observe the cells. Write the names of the stages in correct sequence below.

_____

_____

_____

_____

_____

4 Using the microscope, find one cell representing each stage of cell division. Draw a sketch of each cell and label the stage. You may find it helpful to switch to high power when you are observing the cells to make sketches.

5 With the objective of your microscope at low power, choose an area of the root tip consisting of 50–60 cells. Count the number of cells present in each stage of cell division within your chosen group of cells. Then calculate the percentage value of the number of cells in each stage of cell division that you recorded. Add these values to your data table. Construct a data table in the space below to record your results.

Exploration Lab continued

ANALYZE THE RESULTS

6 **Analyzing Data** Were there any stages of cell division that you did not observe in your group of 50–60 cells? Why might there be a stage that is not represented?

_____
_____
_____
_____

7 **Analyzing Data** What type of graph—line graph, bar graph, or circle graph—would be best to use to make a visual representation of the data in your table? Explain why you chose this graph type.

_____
_____
_____
_____
_____

8 **Making Graphs** Use your data to construct the type of graph you chose in Step 7.

DRAW CONCLUSIONS

9 **Interpreting Results** From your results, which stage of the cell cycle takes the longest time period to complete? What did you notice about the other stages you observed? Explain how you came to this conclusion.

_____
_____
_____
_____

Connect TO THE ESSENTIAL QUESTION

10 **Explaining Concepts** Why does a cell follow a specific pattern of change as it divides?

_____
_____
_____
_____

EXPLORATION LAB INDEPENDENT *Inquiry*

The Stages of the Cell Cycle

A cell passes through specific stages as it divides to form two daughter cells. Taken together, these stages make up the cell cycle. These events are considered cyclic because each generation of cells passes through the same cell cycle as the previous generation.

Each stage requires a different amount of time to complete. If you were to take a snapshot of a group of actively dividing cells, you would find a representative distribution of cells in each stage of the cell cycle. The number of cells you see in each stage gives an indication of how long a period of time the cell spends at that stage. For example, you would find very few cells at a stage that takes a very short time to complete, while you would find a large number of cells at a stage that takes a very long time to complete.

In this lab you will observe a stained microscope slide of actively dividing cells from an onion root tip. You will identify cells in each stage of the cell cycle and count the total number of cells you find at each stage. You can then construct a graph to show this distribution of cells across the stages of the cell cycle and draw conclusions about how long each stage takes to complete.

PROCEDURE

ASK A QUESTION

❶ In this lab, you will investigate the following question: How much time does a cell spend in each stage of the cell cycle?

DEVELOP A PLAN

❷ Work with your partner to make a plan for answering the question in Step 1. Plan to use observations that you make under your microscope of actively dividing plant cells. Summarize your plan below. Obtain your teacher's approval before implementing your plan.

_____

_____

_____

_____

_____

_____

OBJECTIVES

• Identify the stages of the cell cycle from observations of a stained sample of onion root tip tissue.

• Count the number of cells representing each stage and use the data to draw conclusions about the length of time a cell spends at each stage.

MATERIALS

For each student pair

• microscope
• microscope slide
• paper, graphing
• prepared onion root tip tissue

For each student

• safety goggles

Exploration Lab continued

MAKE OBSERVATIONS

❸ Carry out your plan for answering the question from Step 1. Be sure to use an organized method for recording your data and observations.

ANALYZE THE RESULTS

❹ **Analyzing Data** Were there any stages of cell division that you did not observe during your data collection process? Why might there be a stage that is not represented?

_____

_____

_____

_____

❺ **Analyzing Data** What type of graph—line graph, bar graph, or circle graph—would be best to use to make a visual representation of your results? Explain why you chose this graph type.

_____

_____

_____

_____

_____

Exploration Lab continued

6 **Making Graphs** Use your data to construct the type of graph you chose in Step 5.

DRAW CONCLUSIONS

7 **Interpreting Results** From your results, which stage of the cell cycle takes the longest time period to complete? Which stage takes the shortest time to complete? Explain how you drew each of these conclusions.

_____

_____

_____

_____

_____

Connect **TO THE ESSENTIAL QUESTION**

8 **Explaining Concepts** Why does a cell follow a specific pattern of change as it divides?

_____

_____

_____

_____

Meiosis Flipbooks General

👥 Small groups
🕐 20 minutes

LAB RATINGS

LESS ←————————→ MORE

Teacher Prep —

Student Setup —

Cleanup —

SAFETY INFORMATION

Remind students to review all safety cautions and icons before beginning this lab. Warn students that paper brads are sharp and could cause puncture wounds.

TEACHER NOTES

In this activity, students will model the gradual transitions throughout meiosis by making a flipbook. To save time, you may choose to have students punch holes in their cards in advance. It may be necessary to provide textbooks or some other reference for students during this activity so that they can look up the steps of meiosis.

Tip This lab may help students understand the process of meiosis.

Student Tip Try to keep your drawings in the same position on each card.

Skills Focus Making Models, Applying Concepts

MODIFICATION FOR GUIDED *Inquiry*

Provide students with the materials listed, and ask them to make a flipbook showing the events of meiosis. If students are not certain of the steps of meiosis, refer them to their textbooks.

MATERIALS

For each group
- colored pencils, 2 shades of 1 color
- hole punch
- index cards (22)
- paper brads (2)

For each student
- safety goggles

My Notes

_____

_____

_____

_____

_____

Answer Key

6. anaphase I

7. Cards should be labeled "diploid" up until telophase I, at which point the daughter cells are haploid. Telophase I and all of the meiosis II cards are haploid.
Teacher Prompt Think about whether the cell has *two chromosomes*, or *two copies* of *one chromosome*.

11. 4

12. During meiosis, four genetically different haploid cells are produced in the sexual structures of each parent. The haploid cells contain copies of each parent's chromosomes. During fertilization, haploid cells from both parents combine, forming a diploid cell. The diploid cell (offspring) contains chromosomes from each parent.

Meiosis Flipbooks

The process of meiosis involves eight steps, but the transition from one step to the next involves many intermediate stages. In this activity, you will illustrate and assemble a flipbook to show the steps and intermediate stages of meiosis.

PROCEDURE

1 Hold an **index card** horizontally, and use a **hole punch** to put holes in the upper- and lower-left corners of the card. Repeat this step for all of the cards in your pile, trying to line up the holes as closely as possible.

2 Choose one index card. Hold it horizontally and write "Prophase I" at the top.

3 On the index card, have someone from your group draw a single diploid cell as it appears in meiotic prophase I. Keep in mind that your cell has only one pair of homologous chromosomes. Throughout your flipbook, use **colored pencils** to color the homologous chromosomes two different shades of the same color. For example, if you color your homologous chromosomes blue, color one of them light blue and the other dark blue.

4 Divide the remaining index cards among your group. You will now make a flipbook showing the progression of meiosis. Decide who in the group will draw each of the remaining steps. Include metaphase I, anaphase I, telophase I/cytokinesis, prophase II, metaphase II, anaphase II, and telophase II/cytokinesis.

5 Illustrate your assigned steps of meiosis. Be sure to use a separate card for each step, and label the step at the top of the card.

6 As a group, discuss when homologous chromosomes separate. Write "Homologous chromosomes separate" on the appropriate card.

7 In the lower-left corner of each of the cards, indicate whether the cell on that card is haploid or diploid.

8 Arrange your cards in order. Add two blank cards between each of the steps. Use these new cards to illustrate the transition from one step to the next.

OBJECTIVE

- Describe the process of meiosis.

MATERIALS

For each group
- colored pencils, 2 shades of 1 color
- hole punch
- index cards (22)
- paper brads (2)

For each student
- safety goggles

Quick Lab continued

9 Once everyone in your group has finished his or her illustrations, combine the cards to make one flipbook. Fasten the cards together with **paper brads.**

10 Use your completed flipbook to observe the cell as it undergoes meiosis.

11 How many cells are on the last page of your flipbook?

_____

12 What is the relationship between meiosis and the transmission of genetic information from parent to offspring?

_____

_____

_____

_____

_____

_____

_____

_____

_____

_____

_____

_____

_____

_____

_____

_____

_____

_____

_____

QUICK LAB DIRECTED *Inquiry*

Crossover and Meiosis ADVANCED

👥 Student pairs
🕐 15 minutes

LAB RATINGS

LESS ◄─────────► MORE

Teacher Prep —
Student Setup —
Cleanup —

MATERIALS

For each pair
• clay, red, yellow, blue, and green (2 balls of each)
• knife, plastic
For each student
• lab apron
• safety goggles

SAFETY INFORMATION

Remind students to review all safety cautions and icons before beginning this lab. Caution students that even plastic knives can cause injury and should be handled with care.

My Notes

_____
_____
_____
_____

TEACHER NOTES

In this activity, students will model crossing over, meiosis, and fertilization using four colors of clay. Colors other than those listed can be used as long as the colors are different enough that they can be distinguished when they are twisted together.

Tip This activity may help students better understand the crossing over event of meiosis.

Student Tip Pay attention to where the exchange of DNA occurs both before and after fertilization.

Skills Focus Making Models, Drawing Conclusions, Making Predictions

MODIFICATION FOR GUIDED *Inquiry*

Give students various colors of clay, and ask them to demonstrate how genetic material exchanges during meiosis. If students need guidance, encourage them to think through the phases of meiosis and at what point the chromosomes align. Once students have recombined their model chromosomes, have them break them into gametes and conduct "crosses" with other students' gametes. Encourage students to observe the diversity that results.

Answer Key

8. Sample answer: No, they have different amounts of each color of clay.

9. Sample answer: Some of them are very similar, but none of them are exactly the same. There are different combinations of colors of clay.

10. Sample answer: Offspring get two sets of chromosomes due to fertilization, and crossing over ensures that each set contains a mix of chromosomes from each of the parents.

11. The descendants may differ a great deal genetically compared to the original parents.

QUICK LAB DIRECTED Inquiry

Crossover and Meiosis

In this lab, you will use clay to demonstrate the crossing over of chromosomes during meiosis.

PROCEDURE

1 Have one partner start with **2 red and 2 green balls of clay**. Have the other partner start with **2 blue and 2 yellow balls of clay**.

2 Roll each ball of clay into a short rope.

3 Attach pairs of clay ropes at their centers so that you have a pair of each color.

4 Set your pairs of clay ropes (chromosomes) next to each other so that they touch. Twist together the arms that touch.

5 With a **plastic knife**, slice the twisted chromosome arms in half vertically, so that each chromosome has a complete set of arms, but one side is a mixture of the two colors.

6 Divide your chromosome pairs into individual clay ropes again so that you end up with four separate clay ropes. These represent four gametes.

7 Join each one of your clay ropes with one from your partner. This process represents fertilization.

8 Are any of the joined sets of chromosomes the same?

_____

_____

_____

_____

_____

_____

_____

OBJECTIVE

• Model the crossing over of chromosomes during meiosis.

MATERIALS

For each student pair
• clay, red, yellow, blue, and green (2 balls of each)
• knife, plastic

For each student
• lab apron
• safety goggles

Quick Lab continued

9 Compare chromosomes with the rest of the class. How are they different from one another? Are any two the same?

_____

_____

_____

_____

10 How do each of the two events you illustrated, crossing over and fertilization, contribute to genetic diversity in the offspring of your cross?

_____

_____

_____

_____

_____

_____

_____

11 The offspring represented by the clay have small genetic differences compared to their parents. How will the genetic differences compare to the original parents when the offspring reproduce?

_____

_____

_____

_____

_____

QUICK LAB DIRECTED Inquiry

Reproduction and Diversity GENERAL

👥 Individual student

🕐 20 minutes

LAB RATINGS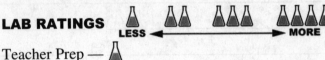

Teacher Prep —

Student Setup —

Cleanup —

MATERIALS

For each student
- coins (6)
- colored pencils
- marker
- paper, blank (2 sheets)
- safety goggles
- tape, masking

SAFETY INFORMATION

Remind students to review all safety cautions and icons before beginning this lab.

TEACHER NOTES

In this activity, students will predict genotypes and phenotypes of the offspring of a fictional species that can reproduce both sexually and asexually. They will then use their predicted offspring to determine how each type of reproduction impacts species diversity.

Skills Focus Making Models, Comparing Results

MODIFICATION FOR GUIDED Inquiry

Give students the listed materials and the genetic information. Have them work in groups to develop and execute a plan for comparing the effects of sexual and asexual reproduction on population diversity. Have groups discuss their methods and results.

My Notes

_____

_____

_____

_____

Answer Key

2. *EEaann* and *Eeaann*

4. *EeAaNn* only

5. Drawings should show three eyes, curly antennae, and a blue nose.

7. *EE*, *Ee*, or *ee*; *AA*, *Aa*, or *aa*; *NN*, *Nn*, or *nn*

10. Answers will vary.

11. Sample answer: The offspring from asexual reproduction looks exactly the same as the parent. The offspring from sexual reproduction looks similar, but not identical, to the parents and the offspring from asexual reproduction.

12. Sample answer: All of the *B. strangus* produced asexually look exactly the same; there is no diversity. The offspring from the sexual crosses, however, have a large variety of phenotypes.

QUICK LAB **DIRECTED** *Inquiry*

Reproduction and Diversity

In this lab, you will predict the genotypes and phenotypes resulting from the sexual and asexual reproduction of a fictional species. You will then compare the effects that each type of reproduction has on population diversity.

PROCEDURE

1 Consider an imaginary animal, *B. strangus*, that can reproduce both asexually and sexually. Examine the information provided below describing the genetics of several of *B. strangus*'s traits.

Trait	Dominant Allele (Symbol)	Recessive Allele (Symbol)
number of eyes	3 eyes *(E)*	2 eyes *(e)*
antenna shape	curly antennae *(A)*	straight antennae *(a)*
nose color	blue nose *(N)*	green nose *(n)*

2 What are all the possible genotypes that can lead to an individual with three eyes, straight antennae, and a green nose?

_____

_____

_____

3 At the top of a separate piece of **paper**, write "Asexual Reproduction." Below the heading, write "parent genotype: *EeAaNn*."

4 List all possible genotypes of the offspring that would result from the asexual reproduction of a *B. strangus* with the genotype *EeAaNn*.

_____

_____

_____

_____

_____

_____

OBJECTIVE

• Compare the effects of sexual and asexual reproduction on genetic diversity.

MATERIALS

For each student
• coins (6)
• colored pencils
• marker
• paper, blank (2 sheets)
• safety goggles
• tape, masking

Quick Lab continued

5 Select one of the genotypes you listed in Step 4. On your sheet of paper, write the genotype and label it "offspring genotype." **Use colored pencils** to draw the offspring with the genotype you chose.

6 At the top of a new piece of paper, write "Sexual Reproduction." Below the heading, write "parental cross *EeAaNn* × *EeAaNn*."

7 List all possible genotypes for each trait of the offspring from the cross described in Step 6.

_____

_____

_____

8 Recall that the probability of passing on an allele is like a coin toss. Use **masking tape** and a **marker** to make a set of **three coins** to represent the alleles of the mother. For example, one coin should have *E* on one side and *e* on the other side.

9 Make another set of coins to represent the alleles of the father.

10 Toss all six coins to determine the genotype of one offspring. Record the genotype and draw the offspring on the paper titled "Sexual Reproduction."

11 How do the offspring of each type of reproduction compare to the parent(s) and to each other?

_____

_____

_____

_____

12 Look at the offspring drawn by some of your classmates. How do the offspring produced by asexual reproduction compare to the ones produced by sexual reproduction?

_____

_____

_____

_____

_____

_____

QUICK LAB DIRECTED *Inquiry*

Egg vs. Sperm BASIC

👥 Student pairs

🕐 25 minutes

LAB RATINGS

LESS ◄─────────► MORE

Teacher Prep —

Student Setup —

Cleanup —

MATERIALS

For each pair

- human egg cell slide
- human sperm cell slide
- microscope
- paper

SAFETY INFORMATION

Remind students to review all safety cautions and icons before beginning this lab. Microscope slides are made of glass and, if broken, can have sharp edges that can cause serious injury. Students should report slide breakages immediately. Glass on the floor can be a slipping hazard. All broken glass should be cleared immediately.

TEACHER NOTES

In this activity, students will observe a human sperm and egg, compare the two cell types, and draw connections between the cells' form and function. If students are unfamiliar with the use of microscopes, you may need to instruct them on how to properly adjust the field of vision.

Skills Focus Practicing Lab Techniques, Making Observations, Drawing Conclusions

My Notes

_____

_____

_____

_____

_____

MODIFICATION FOR GUIDED *Inquiry*

Have students research the size relationship between human sperm and human eggs. Have them brainstorm different ways of modeling this size relationship using everyday objects. Have them write out proposed procedures for modeling this size relationship using everyday objects. Allow students to carry out any reasonable procedures and to record their observations. Encourage them to identify similarities and differences between their models and actual human gametes.

Answer Key

3. Sample answer: 1,000×

4. Answers may vary.

6. Sample answer: 50×

7. Answers may vary.

8. Answers may vary.

9. Sample answer: Egg cells are large because they have to have nutrients to feed the growing zygote before it implants in the uterus.

10. Sample answer: The sperm's tail allows it to swim and propel itself into the egg.

QUICK LAB DIRECTED *Inquiry*

Egg vs. Sperm

In this lab, you will compare size, structure, and function of human gametes by making observations of human sperm cells and human egg cells under a microscope.

PROCEDURE

1 Obtain a **human egg cell slide** and a **human sperm cell slide** from your teacher.

2 Look at the human sperm cell slide under the **microscope.**

3 What magnification must you use to see the sperm cell clearly?

_____

4 In the space below, draw a picture of the sperm cell.

5 Look at the human egg cell slide under the microscope.

6 What magnification must you use to see the egg cell clearly?

_____

7 In the space below, draw a picture of the egg cell.

OBJECTIVES
- Compare the size of a human sperm cell and a human egg cell.
- Describe the relationship between human gamete structure and function.

MATERIALS
For each pair
- human egg cell slide
- human sperm cell slide
- microscope
- paper

8 How does the size of the egg cell compare to the size of the sperm cell?

_____

_____

9 Why do you think it is important for the egg cell to be so large?

_____

_____

_____

10 How does the structure of the sperm cell enable it to perform its function?

_____

_____

QUICK LAB GUIDED *Inquiry*

QUICK LAB GUIDED *Inquiry*

Create a Classification System GENERAL

👥 Small groups
🕐 20 minutes/day for 2 days

LAB RATINGS

🧪 🧪🧪 🧪🧪🧪 🧪🧪🧪🧪
LESS ⟵——————————⟶ MORE

Teacher Prep — 🧪🧪

Student Setup — 🧪

Cleanup — 🧪

MATERIALS

For each group
- compass or protractor
- index cards
- markers
- paper
- pencils
- poster board
- ruler
- sample classification systems/tools

TEACHER NOTES

In this lab, students will create systems to classify organisms by their reproductive processes. Collect several examples of classification tools, such as dichotomous keys and field guides, for students to use as models. Students will work in groups to design, test, and troubleshoot their own classification systems. Ask students questions to elicit ideas about how classification systems in general work, such as "Do you need to determine what the least inclusive categories should be before you design your classification system?" Guide students to the realization that if an organism could be classified into more than one group, then the system may be flawed or incomplete.

Skills Focus Identifying Patterns, Classifying Information, Comparing Models

My Notes

_____

_____

_____

_____

_____

MODIFICATION FOR DIRECTED *Inquiry*

Instead of having groups choose classification systems, have all groups create dichotomous keys. You may also wish to give them as their classification endpoints the following categories: bird, mammal, reptile, amphibian, fish, flowering plant, fungus, and bacterium.

Answer Key

2. Answers will vary.

3. Answers will vary, but students should recognize that a hierarchy within a classification system allows for clustering related individuals or groups into larger groups.

4. Answers will vary.

5. Answers will vary.

6. Answers will vary.

7. Answers will vary.

QUICK LAB GUIDED *Inquiry*

Create a Classification System

In this lab, you will create a system to classify different organisms by the processes they use to reproduce. Scientists use classification systems to group organisms by their properties.

PROCEDURE

❶ Examine the **sample classification systems** provided by your teacher.

❷ Brainstorm a list of reproductive processes used by organisms, including different types of plants, animals, fungi, protists, and bacteria.

_____

_____

_____

_____

❸ Do any of the processes you identified seem more closely related to one another than to other processes? Which ones? How could you develop a system that would take these possible relationships into account?

_____

_____

_____

_____

❹ Work with your group to design a system to classify organisms by the processes they use to reproduce. Use the materials provided to draw, write out, or build your classification system so other groups can follow it easily.

OBJECTIVE

• Compare and contrast the general processes of sexual reproduction and asexual reproduction.

MATERIALS

For each group

• compass or protractor
• index cards
• markers
• paper
• pencils
• poster board
• ruler
• sample classification systems

Quick Lab continued

5 Test and troubleshoot your classification system. Choose a variety of organisms to classify using your system. Did your system result in correct classifications based on what you already know about each organism? Note any difficulties and record your ideas. Then, make changes to your classification system as necessary.

_____

_____

_____

_____

_____

_____

6 Try out the classification systems created by other groups for the organisms you selected. How are these systems similar to the one your group created?

_____

_____

_____

_____

7 How do the systems created by other groups differ from the one your group created? Do any help you classify the organisms more easily? Do any make it more difficult to classify the organisms?

_____

_____

_____

_____

_____

_____

_____

_____

Investigate Asexual Reproduction GENERAL

👥 Student Pairs

🕐 Three 45-minute class periods

LAB RATINGS

LESS ◄————————► MORE

Teacher Prep —

Student Setup —

Cleanup —

MATERIALS

For each pair
- containers
- cuttings from local native plants
- geranium plant
- notebook
- scissors
- soil, potting
- sweet potato tuber

For each student
- lab apron
- safety goggles

SAFETY INFORMATION

Remind students to review all safety cautions and icons before beginning this lab. Have students pay particular attention to the guidelines for safety in field investigations. Be sure students know they might encounter plants and animals which are harmful and that they can identify these organisms and avoid all contact with them. Be sure to learn in advance whether any students have known allergies to plants or to bee stings, and take any necessary precautions. Students should be instructed to wash their hands after completing the activity.

TEACHER NOTES

In this activity, students will collect cuttings of local plants to bring back to the lab for propagation. Care will be taken to obtain appropriate permissions before taking any plant materials and to refrain from harming plants. Upon returning to the lab, students will work in pairs to set up conditions in which to test the plant parts to observe whether they will grow into new plants. For comparison purposes, students will set up propagation experiments using geranium leaves and sweet potato tubers, both of which are fairly easy to propagate.

Tip This lab may help students understand that some parts of plants are better able to propagate asexually than other parts of plants.

Student Tip Consider that different parts of plants may differ in their ability to propagate.

Skills Focus Practicing Lab Techniques, Recording Observations, Drawing Conclusions

MODIFICATION FOR DIRECTED Inquiry

For the directed inquiry version of this lab, show students how to make cuttings at various points along the petiole of leaf (for example, including some stem along with the entire petiole, cutting midway along the petiole, and cutting close to the leaf to omit the petiole). Assist students with organizing and labeling their experiments and recording their observations.

My Notes

_____

_____

_____

_____

_____

Field Lab continued

Answer Key for GUIDED Inquiry

ASK A QUESTION

1. Accept any reasonable answer.

Teacher Prompt What kinds of growing conditions might native plants need compared to a geranium and a sweet potato tuber?

IDENTIFY A PROBLEM

2. Accept any reasonable answer.

Teacher Prompt If we can propagate geranium and sweet potato tuber with cuttings, what type of propagation might be the best way to conserve native plants?

DEVELOP A PLAN

3. Sample answer: We could compare the ability of different plants and plant parts to propagate asexually by comparing the ability of different parts of plants and different types of plants to propagate. Be sure to include some stem in addition to the entire petiole.

Teacher Prompt Why are we using geranium *and* sweet potato tuber as experimental plants in our observations of propagation? What parts of the plant might propagate better than others?

ANALYZE THE RESULTS

6. Accept any reasonable answer.

Teacher Prompt What features of plant growth did you use to assess the ability of plant types and plant parts to propagate?

DRAW CONCLUSIONS

7. Accept any reasonable answer.

Teacher Prompt Do native plants propagate easily, or did you have trouble getting the native plants to propagate?

Connect TO THE ESSENTIAL QUESTION

8. Sample answer: Asexual reproduction may be advantageous because it is faster than sexual reproduction and it does not require pollination.

Teacher Prompt How long does a plant take to grow from seed produced by sexual reproduction compared with propagation by asexual reproduction? How is a seed produced from flowers?

Answer Key for INDEPENDENT Inquiry

ASK A QUESTION

1. Accept any reasonable answer.

Teacher Prompt What kinds of growing conditions might native plants need compared with geranium and sweet potato tuber?

IDENTIFY A PROBLEM

2. Accept any reasonable answer.

Teacher Prompt If we can propagate geranium and sweet potato tuber with cuttings, what type of propagation might be the best way to conserve native plants?

DEVELOP A PLAN

3. Sample answer: We could compare the ability of different plants and plant parts to propagate asexually by comparing the ability of different parts of plants and different types of plants to propagate. You could make cuttings in different ways to see if one way of making a cutting worked better than other ways.

Teacher Prompt Why are we using geranium *and* sweet potato tuber as experimental plants in our observations of propagation?

ANALYZE THE RESULTS

6. Accept any reasonable answer.

Teacher Prompt What features of plant growth did you use to assess the ability of plant types and plant parts to propagate?

DRAW CONCLUSIONS

7. Accept any reasonable answer.

Teacher Prompt Do native plants propagate easily, or did you have trouble getting the native plants to propagate?

Connect TO THE ESSENTIAL QUESTION

8. Sample answer: Asexual reproduction may be advantageous because it is faster than sexual reproduction and it does not require pollination.

Teacher Prompt How long does a plant take to grow from seed produced by sexual reproduction compared with propagation by asexual reproduction? How is a seed produced from flowers?

FIELD LAB GUIDED *Inquiry*

Investigate Asexual Reproduction

In this lab, you will take cuttings of plants to bring back to the lab for propagation. Work in pairs to test various plant parts to observe whether they will grow into new plants.

PROCEDURE

ASK A QUESTION

1 Since most plants have some ability to reproduce asexually, how do you think native plants will differ, if at all, from geranium and sweet potato tuber in their ability to propagate from various plant parts?

_____

_____

IDENTIFY A PROBLEM

2 How can we conserve rare native plants compared with cultivated plants?

_____

_____

DEVELOP A PLAN

3 How might you compare the ability of different plants and plant parts to propagate asexually? You will need to take cuttings of the geranium plant to include a portion of stem with the leaf petiole. For the tuber, find an "eye" (a small indentation) in the side of the tuber. Cut a flat section of the tuber around this indentation and plant with the skin facing up.

_____

_____

_____

_____

OBJECTIVES

- Gather cuttings from local native plants to test whether they can propagate vegetatively, including samples of various organs including leaves, stems, and roots.
- Compare results to the propagation of geranium plants and sweet potato tubers.

MATERIALS

For each student pair
- containers
- cuttings from local native plants
- geranium plant
- notebook
- scissors
- soil, potting
- sweet potato tuber

For each student
- lab apron
- safety goggles

Field Lab continued

IMPLEMENT THE PLAN

4 Take cuttings of various parts of the geranium plant, the potato tuber, and the native plants. Place in the potting soil and water gently. Do not soak the soil.

MAKE OBSERVATIONS

5 Over the next few weeks observe your cuttings closely. Record your observations in your notebook. Be sure to keep the samples appropriately moist.

ANALYZE THE RESULTS

6 **Comparing Observations** How do the various plant parts compare in their ability to propagate? How do different plants compare in their ability to propagate?

_____

_____

_____

_____

DRAW CONCLUSIONS

7 **Interpreting Observations** If one kind of plant or part of a plant propagates more readily than another, what can you conclude about propagation as a way to conserve native plants?

_____

_____

Connect TO THE ESSENTIAL QUESTION

8 **Applying Conclusions** Describe in what way asexual reproduction may be advantageous to a plant.

_____

_____

_____

_____

FIELD LAB INDEPENDENT *Inquiry*

Investigate Asexual Reproduction

In this lab, you will take cuttings of plants to bring back to the lab for propagation. Work in pairs to test various plant parts to observe whether they will grow into new plants.

PROCEDURE

ASK A QUESTION

❶ Since most plants have some ability to reproduce asexually, how do you think native plants will differ, if at all, from geranium and sweet potato tuber in their ability to propagate from various plant parts?

_____

_____

IDENTIFY A PROBLEM

❷ How can we conserve rare native plants compared with cultivated plants?

_____

_____

DEVELOP A PLAN

❸ How might you compare the ability of different plants and plant parts to propagate asexually? Will taking cuttings in different ways increase the likelihood the cutting will grow?

_____

_____

_____

OBJECTIVES
• Gather cuttings from local native plants to test whether they can propagate vegetatively, including samples of various organs including leaves, stems, and roots.
• Compare results to the propagation of geranium plants and sweet potato tubers.

MATERIALS
For each student pair
• containers
• cuttings from local native plants
• geranium plant
• notebook
• scissors
• soil, potting
• sweet potato tuber
For each student
• lab apron
• safety goggles

Field Lab continued

IMPLEMENT THE PLAN

④ Take cuttings of various parts of the geranium plant, the potato tuber, and the native plants. Place in the potting soil and water gently. Do not soak the soil.

MAKE OBSERVATIONS

⑤ Over the next few weeks observe your cuttings closely. Record your observations in your notebook. Be sure to keep the samples appropriately moist.

ANALYZE THE RESULTS

⑥ **Comparing Observations** How do the various plant parts compare in their ability to propagate? How do different plants compare in their ability to propagate?

_____

_____

_____

_____

DRAW CONCLUSIONS

⑦ **Interpreting Observations** If one kind of plant or part of a plant propagates more readily than another, what can you conclude about propagation as a way to conserve native plants? Would making the cuttings in one particular way change your conclusion?

_____

_____

Connect **TO THE ESSENTIAL QUESTION**

⑧ **Applying Conclusions** Describe in what way asexual reproduction may be advantageous to a plant.

_____

_____

_____

_____

QUICK LAB GUIDED *Inquiry*

Dominant Alleles ADVANCED

👥 Small groups

🕐 20 minutes

LAB RATINGS

LESS ◄——————► MORE

Teacher Prep —

Student Setup —

Cleanup —

MATERIALS

For each group
- index cards or card stock (5)
- marker, red
- marker, yellow
- paper, white
- plastic wrap, clear
- ruler
- scissors
- tape

For each student
- safety goggles

SAFETY INFORMATION

Remind students to review all safety cautions and icons before beginning this lab. Caution students that scissors are sharp and can cause injury.

TEACHER NOTES

In this activity, students will use colored plastic wrap to demonstrate different patterns of inheritance. They will experiment with color combinations to represent complete dominance, incomplete dominance, and codominance.

Tip This activity may help students understand the difference between complete dominance, incomplete dominance, and codominance.

Student Tip Instead of making a fifth frame, just use the clear one from Step 3

Skills Focus Making Models, Interpreting Data, Applying Concepts

MODIFICATION FOR DIRECTED *Inquiry*

Instead of having students figure out how to represent each form of dominance, tell them which frames to hold together and ask them to identify which form of dominance the combination shows.

My Notes

_____

_____

_____

_____

_____

Answer Key

6. Sample answer: I put a clear frame and a yellow frame together. I see yellow.

7. Sample answer: I put a red frame and a yellow frame together. I see orange. My prediction was correct.

8. Sample answer: I divided each frame into quadrants. In the first frame, I colored the top-left and bottom-right quadrants red. In the second one, I colored the top-right and bottom-left quadrants yellow. When I hold them together, some areas are red and some are yellow.

9. This lab models inherited traits that living things have when they are born. Acquired and learned traits are characteristics that living things gain after they are born.

QUICK LAB GUIDED Inquiry

Dominant Alleles

In this lab, you will use colored plastic wrap to demonstrate different patterns of inheritance.

PROCEDURE

① Make three frames. To make a frame, use a **ruler** to draw a 5 cm × 5 cm square in the center of an **index card.** Use **scissors** to cut out the square. Try not to bend the card.

② Use tape to fasten **clear plastic wrap** to the back of each frame.

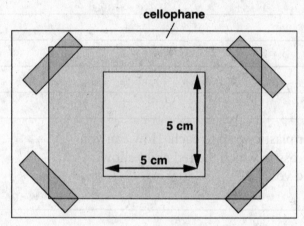

cellophane

5 cm

5 cm

③ Use **markers** to color the plastic wrap on two frames. Color one red and one yellow, and leave the last one clear.

④ Now use your frames to represent the results of genetic crosses. Imagine that yellow and red are each alleles of a gene that determines color.

⑤ Lay the red frame over the clear frame, and hold them over a piece of **white paper**. You should see red when you look through the aligned frames. This frame combination represents a cross in which the red allele is completely dominant (and the clear allele, therefore, is recessive).

OBJECTIVE
• Describe the difference between complete dominance, incomplete dominance, and codominance.

MATERIALS
For each group
• index cards or card stock (5)
• marker, red
• marker, yellow
• paper, white
• plastic wrap, clear
• ruler
• scissors
• tape
For each student
• safety goggles

Quick Lab continued

6 How can you use your frames to represent a cross in which the yellow allele is completely dominant? Look through the frames. What do you see?

_____

_____

_____

7 Predict how you can use your frames to represent a cross in which there is incomplete dominance. What do you see? Was your prediction correct?

_____

_____

_____

_____

_____

8 Make two new frames, and attach clear plastic wrap to each. How can you color and use these frames to show a cross in which the red and yellow alleles are codominant? Try it. What do you see?

_____

_____

_____

_____

9 Are the traits that you are modeling in this lab inherited, acquired, or learned? Explain.

_____

_____

_____

_____

144

QUICK LAB DIRECTED *Inquiry*

What's the Difference Between a Dominant Trait and a Recessive Trait? GENERAL

👥 Student pairs
🕐 20 minutes

LAB RATINGS

LESS ◄————————► MORE

Teacher Prep —

Student Setup —

Cleanup —

MATERIALS

For each student pair
- bag, paper lunch
- beads, 2 colors (6 of each color)
- paper
- pencil

My Notes

_____
_____
_____
_____
_____

TEACHER NOTES

In this activity, student pairs work with a model to study dominant and recessive alleles and the conditions under which they are expressed. Inform students that one bead color (for example, blue) represents a dominant allele and will be represented by a capital B. The other bead color (for example, green) represents a recessive allele and will be represented by a lower case b. Tell students that two blue beads, BB, OR a blue and a green bead, Bb, results in a blue flower. Two green beads, bb, represent a green flower. Students will draw two beads at random to represent the maternal genotype of the parent generation. They will remove two beads at random to represent the paternal genotype of the parent generation. Using the parental alleles, the students will simulate a monohybrid cross to generate F1 genotypes. They will then cross the alleles from two of the offspring produced from the F1 cross to generate F2 genotypes. Thus, students will be able to establish the phenotypic ratios in an F2 generation given specific parent phenotypes. If one parent (parent generation) is homozygous dominant and the other is homozygous recessive, students will conclude that there is a 3:1 Mendelian phenotypic ratio produced in the F2 generation.

Tip This activity will help students understand that a dominant allele will mask the expression of a recessive allele.

Skills Focus Applying Concepts, Developing Models, Comparing Data

MODIFICATION FOR GUIDED *Inquiry*

Allow students to choose which color beads to use as the dominant allele and which to use as the recessive allele.

Answer Key

1. Students should specify which color bead represents which allele. (for example, blue represents a dominant allele and green represents the recessive allele.)

2. Sample answer: Two blue alleles or a blue and green allele result in the dominant trait.
   Teacher Prompt What does a dominant allele do to a recessive allele?

3. Sample answer: Two green alleles result in the recessive trait, resulting in the green phenotype.
   Teacher Prompt If the dominant allele suppresses expression of the recessive allele, what will happen if there are no dominant alleles present?

4. Sample answer: If a total of four beads are drawn, there are five possible combinations:
   BBBB, BBBb, BBbb, Bbbb, bbbb
   Teacher Prompt If you only remove two beads, how many possible combinations are there?

5. Answers will vary.

6. Answers will vary. See example in table for BB × bb.

		Maternal genotype	
		B	B
Paternal	b	Bb	Bb
genotype	b	Bb	Bb

7. Answers will vary. In the example, the phenotypes are all blue.

8. Answers will vary. See example in table for Bb × Bb.

		Female genotype from F1 cross	
		B	b
Male genotype from F1 cross	B	BB	Bb
	b	Bb	bb

9. Answers will vary. In the example, there are three flowers with the blue phenotypes and one flower with the green phenotype.

10. Answers will vary.

11. Sample answer: The phenotype of all offspring will be blue, or all heterozygous.
    Teacher Prompt What are the phenotypes in the cases of a homozygous dominant genotype and a homozygous recessive genotype?

QUICK LAB DIRECTED *Inquiry*

What's the Difference Between a Dominant Trait and a Recessive Trait?

In this lab you will simulate crosses between different colored flowers. The results of the crosses will help you see patterns of inheritance that involve dominant and recessive traits.

PROCEDURE

❶ Your teacher will tell you what the colored beads represent. Write down which bead represents a dominant allele and which bead represents the recessive allele.

_____

_____

❷ Which pair(s) of alleles will result in the dominant trait showing in the phenotype?

_____

❸ Which pair(s) of alleles will result in the recessive trait showing in the phenotype?

_____

❹ If you remove a total of four beads from the bag, how many combinations of alleles are possible with two colors of beads?

_____

❺ Without looking, remove two beads at random from the bag to represent the maternal genotype. Then remove another two beads at random to represent the paternal genotype. Write down the two pairs of beads you selected.

OBJECTIVE

• Observe the relationship between phenotype and genotype.

MATERIALS

For each student pair
• bag, paper lunch
• beads, 2 colors (6 of each color)
• paper
• pencil

Quick Lab continued

6 Simulate a parental monohybrid cross between the two genotypes by entering the alleles in the gray boxes in the table below (called a Punnett square). When these two parents are crossed, the four possible offspring outcomes (white boxes) represent the F1 generation.

		Maternal genotype	
Paternal genotype			

7 What phenotypes do you see in the F1 generation?

_____

_____

8 Take any two of the genotypes from your table for the F1 generation and simulate another monohybrid cross between the two genotypes by entering the alleles in the table below. This represents the F2 generation.

		Maternal genotype	
Paternal genotype			

9 What phenotypes do you see in the F2 generation?

_____

_____

10 Repeat Steps 5 through 9 until you have simulated several different combinations of alleles (from Step 4). (If you get the same color beads, draw again – you want to cross different genotypes each time.) Create additional Punnett squares on a separate piece of paper if needed.

11 What can you conclude about the F2 phenotypic ratios if one parent is homozygous dominant and the other is homozygous recessive?

_____

_____

QUICK LAB DIRECTED Inquiry

Gender Determination GENERAL

👤 Individual student
🕐 15 minutes

LAB RATINGS

LESS ◄─────────► MORE

Teacher Prep — 🧪
Student Setup — 🧪
Cleanup — 🧪

MATERIALS

For each student
• coin
• paper
• safety goggles

My Notes

_____

_____

_____

_____

_____

SAFETY INFORMATION

Remind students to review all safety cautions and icons before beginning this lab.

TEACHER NOTES

In this activity, students will draw a Punnett square to determine the probability for the gender of the offspring. They will then toss coins to see the actual results of a small number of theoretical crosses.

Tip This activity may help students understand how Punnett squares can be used to determine the likelihood that a particular genetic trait will be passed on to offspring.

Skills Focus Interpreting Data, Making Predictions

MODIFICATION FOR GUIDED Inquiry

Ask students to construct a Punnett square that illustrates the probability of having male or female offspring. Challenge students to design a way to represent the results of random crosses in order to examine the accuracy of their Punnett square's predictions. Encourage students to perform a large number of crosses and to periodically reevaluate the percentage of male and female offspring.

Answer Key

1.–4.

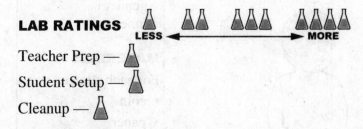

5. 50% male, 50% female

6. Answers will vary.

7. Sample answer: They were not the same because only 25% of the coin tosses produced females, and the Punnett square predicted 50% female offspring. This is probably because I only did 4 coin tosses. If I did 400 tosses, it would be more accurate and would come close to 50%.

QUICK LAB DIRECTED *Inquiry*

Gender Determination

In this lab, you will construct a Punnett square to determine the probability that offspring will inherit X or Y chromosomes from their parents.

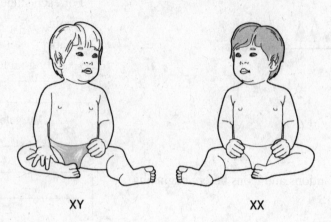

XY   XX

PROCEDURE

1 Draw a Punnett square in the space below.

OBJECTIVE

• Explain how gender is inherited.

MATERIALS

For each student

• coin

• paper

• safety goggles

Quick Lab continued

2 What are the mother's two sex chromosomes? Write them in the appropriate spaces on the Punnett square.

3 What are the father's two sex chromosomes? Write them in the appropriate spaces on the Punnett square.

4 Complete the Punnett square to show the possible genotypes of the offspring.

5 What percentage of the offspring are predicted to be female? Male?

_____

_____

6 Flip a **coin** to represent the inheritance of the father's gamete. If you flip heads, record that result as the inheritance of a Y chromosome. If you flip tails, record it as the inheritance of an X chromosome. Flip the coin 4 times, and record your results.

_____

_____

_____

_____

_____

_____

_____

7 How did the results of your coin toss compare to what was predicted by your Punnett square? How would your answer change if you flipped the coin 400 times? Explain your answer.

_____

_____

_____

_____

_____

_____

Interpreting Pedigree Charts GENERAL

👥 Individual student

🕐 10 min

LAB RATINGS

LESS ◄——————► MORE

Teacher Prep —

Student Setup —

Cleanup —

	MATERIAL
	For each student
	• six-sided die

My Notes

_____

_____

_____

_____

_____

TEACHER NOTES

In this activity, students will interpret and predict traits based on a pedigree chart.

Tip This activity may help students understand how to construct and interpret pedigree charts.

Skills Focus Interpreting Data, Evaluating Models

MODIFICATION FOR GUIDED *Inquiry*

Give students completely blank pedigree charts, and ask them to choose a trait that is recessive or dominant. Have them fill out a portion of their chart however they wish and exchange charts with another student. Each student must then complete the other student's chart based on what information he or she has. Students should then return their charts to the original owners and, as a pair, review the chart to determine whether or not the predicted pattern of inheritance is possible or correct.

Answer Key

3. Answers will vary.
4. Answers will vary.
5. #3 = male; #4 = female; #5 = female; #6 = male
6. Their shapes are black.
7. Their shapes are half black and half white.
8. She is his aunt.

QUICK LAB DIRECTED *Inquiry*

Interpreting Pedigree Charts

In this lab, you will use a pedigree chart to detect the presence or absence of a recessive trait in members of different generations of the same family.

PROCEDURE

1 Use the **six-sided die** to fill out your pedigree chart, which is shown on the next page. Roll the die and color the square for Person 1 according to the result.

1 or 2 = normal

3 or 4 = carrier

5 or 6 = expresses the trait

2 Repeat Step 1 for Person 6 and for Person 8.

3 Based on the information you have for Persons 1, 2, 6, 7, and 8, fill in the circles and squares for Persons 3, 4, and 5.

4 Is there more than one possible result for Persons 3, 4, and 5? Explain your answer.

_____

_____

_____

_____

_____

_____

_____

_____

_____

_____

_____

_____

_____

_____

_____

_____

OBJECTIVES

• Interpret a pedigree chart.

• Predict patterns of inheritance of a recessive trait.

MATERIAL

For each student

• six-sided die

Quick Lab continued

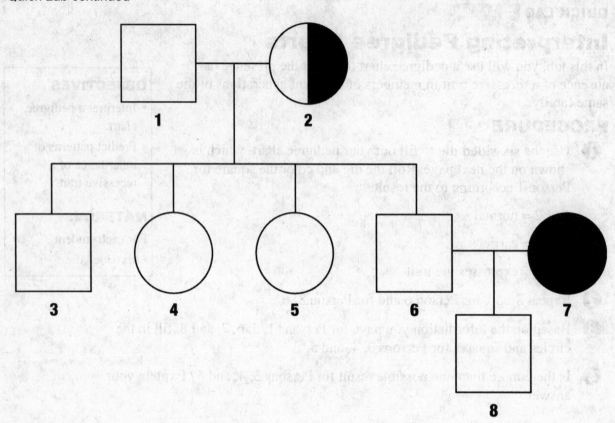

KEY:

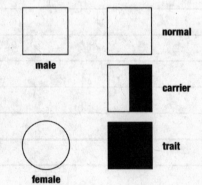

Quick Lab continued

5 What is the gender of each person of the second generation?

_____

_____

_____

_____

_____

6 How can you tell which people have the trait?

_____

_____

_____

_____

_____

_____

7 How can you tell which people are carriers for the trait?

_____

_____

_____

_____

_____

_____

8 What is Person 4's relationship to Person 8?

_____

_____

_____

_____

_____

QUICK LAB DIRECTED Inquiry

Completing a Punnett Square GENERAL

👥 Individual student

🕐 15 minutes

LAB RATINGS

LESS ◄────────► MORE

Teacher Prep —

Student Setup —

Cleanup —

MATERIALS
• no materials required

My Notes
_____
_____
_____
_____
_____

SAFETY INFORMATION

Remind students to review all safety cautions and icons before beginning this lab.

TEACHER NOTES

In this activity, students will construct a Punnett square to predict the genotypes of the offspring resulting from a cross of two heterozygous plants. They will then use their results to predict the offspring's possible phenotypes.

Tip This activity may help students understand how to use Punnett squares, and the relationship between genotype and phenotype.

Skills Focus Interpreting Data, Applying Concepts

MODIFICATION FOR GUIDED Inquiry

Provide students with a list of Mendelian traits and descriptions of the gene controlling each trait, its alleles, and the relative dominance of the alleles. Be sure to choose traits that have only two or three alleles. Some good examples of appropriate human traits to study are the presence or absence of freckles, attached earlobes, cheek dimples, widow's peaks, and cleft chins. Ask students to select a gene from the list and predict the genotypes and phenotypes of offspring produced by a cross of two heterozygous parents.

Answer Key

2.–4.

	R	r
R	RR	Rr
r	Rr	rr

5. *RR, Rr, rr*

6. Complete dominance: *RR* = round; *Rr* = round; *rr* = wrinkled

Incomplete dominance: *RR* = round; *Rr* = slightly wrinkled; *rr* = wrinkled

QUICK LAB DIRECTED Inquiry

Completing a Punnett Square

In this lab, you will use a Punnett square to determine the possible genotypes and phenotypes of the offspring of a genetic cross.

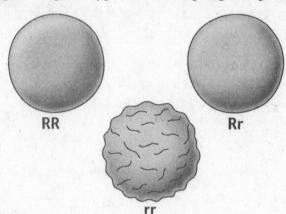

RR   Rr

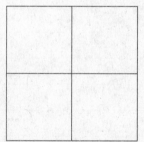

rr

OBJECTIVE

- Use a Punnett square to predict the probabilities of genotypes and phenotypes.

MATERIAL

- no materials required

PROCEDURE

1 The cross shown below is between two plants that produce round seeds. Notice that the genotype for each plant is *Rr*. Round seeds *(R)* are dominant, and wrinkled seeds *(r)* are recessive.

Rr × Rr

2 Use the square below to determine the possible genotypes for this cross. Write "*R*" and "*r*" above the top two boxes, and again to the left of the two boxes on the left side. Each "*Rr*" represents the alleles of one parent from the cross.

3 Fill in each column in the square with the letter on the top of that column.

4 Fill in each row in the square with the letter on the side of that row.

Quick Lab continued

5 List all of the possible genotypes of the offspring from the cross shown on the previous page.

_____

_____

_____

_____

6 What are the possible phenotypes of the offspring from the cross on the previous page if round seeds *(R)* are completely dominant to wrinkled seeds *(r)*? What would the possible phenotypes be if round seeds were incompletely dominant to wrinkled seeds?

_____

_____

_____

_____

_____

_____

_____

_____

_____

_____

_____

_____

_____

_____

_____

_____

_____

_____

S.T.E.M. LAB DIRECTED Inquiry AND GUIDED Inquiry

Matching Punnett Square Predictions GENERAL

👥 Student pairs

🕐 45 minutes

LAB RATINGS

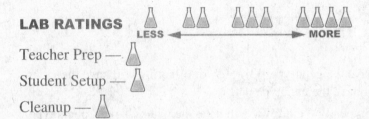

LESS ←——————→ MORE

Teacher Prep —

Student Setup —

Cleanup —

MATERIALS

For each student pair
- marker
- paper, blank
- paper, graphing
- pennies (2)
- tape, masking

For each student
- safety goggles

My Notes

_____

_____

_____

_____

_____

SAFETY INFORMATION

Remind students to review all safety cautions and icons before beginning this lab. Be sure that students wear safety goggles when flipping the pennies to avoid the possibility of eye injury.

TEACHER NOTES

In this activity, students will flip pennies to determine whether the actual outcomes of a genetic cross can be expected to match the outcomes predicted by a Punnett square analysis. Students will discover that if a small number of offspring are counted, there is wide scatter in the resulting offspring genotypes and phenotypes. They will find that the larger the pool of offspring, the closer the match of phenotype and genotype distribution is to that predicted by Punnett square analysis. Class data will be pooled in order for students to observe the scatter in data.

You can omit the step of marking pennies by having students use heads for the dominant gene (W) and tails for the recessive gene (w). You may wish to review how to calculate percentages before students begin this activity.

Tip This lab will give students practice using Punnett squares.

Student Tip Underline the capital W to make it obvious which is the capital.

Skills Focus Pooling Results, Graphing Data, Drawing Conclusions

MODIFICATION FOR INDEPENDENT Inquiry

Students can be instructed to develop their own data tables. They can also examine the pooled class data and make their own decision about the type of graph they would like to use to illustrate the scatter in class data.

S.T.E.M. Lab continued

Answer Key for DIRECTED *Inquiry*

RESEARCH A PROBLEM

2.

	W	w
W	WW	Ww
w	Ww	ww

3. Sample answer: 25% of offspring will have the genotype *WW*, 50% of offspring will have the genotype *Ww*, and 25% of offspring will have the genotype *ww*.

4. Sample answer: Offspring with the genotypes WW and Ww will have the widow's peak phenotype. Offspring with the *ww* genotype will have the straight hairline phenotype.

MAKE OBSERVATIONS

8. Accept all reasonable answers.

9. Accept all reasonable answers.

10.

RESULTS FROM PUNNETT SQUARE ANALYSIS AND COIN TOSSES

	Genotype			Phenotype	
	WW	Ww	ww	Widow's peak	Straight hairline
% predicted	25%	50%	25%	75%	25%
Actual % based on 4 coin tosses	Accept all reasonable answers.				
Actual % based on 100 coin tosses	Accept all reasonable answers.				

11. Accept all reasonable answers.

ANALYZE THE RESULTS

12. Accept all reasonable answers. Check to be sure students are graphing the data they obtained.

13. Accept all reasonable answers. Be sure students are correctly describing the data they obtained.

DRAW CONCLUSIONS

14. Sample answer: Yes, my results allow me to answer the question. Not every cross results in the outcome predicted by the Punnett square analysis. When the number of offspring is very small, there is more scatter in the resulting percentages of phenotypes.

S.T.E.M. Lab continued

Connect **TO THE ESSENTIAL QUESTION**

15. Sample answer: It is best to design a genetic cross experiment so that a very large number of offspring can be counted. Otherwise, the results may not be accurate.

Answer Key for GUIDED Inquiry

RESEARCH A PROBLEM

2.

	W	w
W	WW	Ww
w	Ww	ww

3. Sample answer: 25% of offspring will have the genotype *WW*, 50% of offspring will have the genotype *Ww*, and 25% of offspring will have the genotype *ww*.

4. Sample answer: Offspring with the genotypes WW and Ww will have the widow's peak phenotype. Offspring with the *ww* genotype will have the straight hairline phenotype.

MAKE A PLAN

6. Accept all reasonable answers.

MAKE OBSERVATIONS

7. Accept all reasonable answers.

8. Accept all reasonable answers.

9.

RESULTS FROM PUNNETT SQUARE ANALYSIS AND COIN TOSSES

	Genotype			Phenotype	
	WW	**Ww**	**ww**	**Widow's peak**	**Straight hairline**
% predicted	25%	50%	25%	75%	25%
Actual % based on 4 coin tosses	Accept all reasonable answers.				
Actual % based on 100 coin tosses	Accept all reasonable answers.				

10. Accept all reasonable answers.

ANALYZE THE RESULTS

11. Accept all reasonable answers. Check to be sure students are graphing the data they obtained.

12. Accept all reasonable answers. Be sure students are correctly describing the data they obtained.

DRAW CONCLUSIONS

13. Sample answer: Yes, my results allow me to answer the question. Not every cross results in the outcome predicted by the Punnett square analysis. When the number of offspring is very small, there is more scatter in the resulting percentages of phenotypes.

Connect TO THE ESSENTIAL QUESTION

14. Sample answer: It is best to design a genetic cross experiment so that a very large number of offspring can be counted. Otherwise, the results may not be accurate.

S.T.E.M. LAB DIRECTED Inquiry

Matching Punnett Square Predictions

Punnett squares are used to predict the possible outcomes from the genetic cross of two parents. However, Punnett square analysis assumes that a sizeable number of offspring are produced. In this lab, you will observe the actual distribution of offspring phenotypes from some crosses and also determine the number of offspring necessary to accurately match a Punnett square prediction.

You will follow a human trait during this analysis. The trait involves the shape of the hairline across the top of a person's forehead. If a person has a dominant allele (*W*) for this trait, their hairline forms a distinct point in the middle of the forehead called a widow's peak. People with straight hairlines have two recessive alleles (*w*) for this trait.

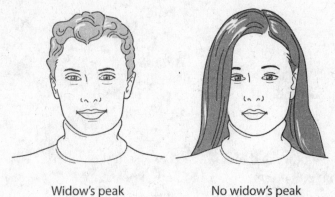

Widow's peak   No widow's peak

OBJECTIVES

- Use a Punnett square to predict the possible outcomes of a genetic cross.
- Compare the results of a simulated genetic cross to the outcomes predicted by a Punnett square.

MATERIALS

For each student pair
- marker
- paper, blank
- paper, graphing
- pennies (2)
- tape, masking

For each student
- safety goggles

PROCEDURE

RESEARCH A PROBLEM

1 On a separate piece of paper, make a Punnett square for two parents who are both heterozygous (*Ww*) for the widow's peak trait.

2 Complete the Punnett square for the offspring.

3 Based on the Punnett square, what percentage of offspring will have the genotypes *WW, Ww,* and *ww*?

_____

_____

_____

S.T.E.M. Lab continued

4 Based on the Punnett square analysis, what are the expected phenotypes of these offspring? What percentage of the offspring is predicted to have a widow's peak? What percentage of the offspring is predicted to have a straight hairline?

_____

_____

_____

_____

ASK A QUESTION

5 A Punnett square analysis can be used to predict the outcomes of a genetic cross. However, does every actual cross always result in the outcome predicted by the Punnett square analysis? You will explore the answer to this question by carrying out your own simulated genetic crosses.

MAKE OBSERVATIONS

6 Put masking tape on both sides of two pennies.

7 Use a marker to write a lowercase w for the straight hairline allele on one side of each penny. Then, write a capital *W* for the widow's peak allele on the other side of each penny. Underline the capital *W* to make it obvious which is the capital.

8 Use one penny to represent the mother and the other to represent the father. "Cross" the parents by flipping both coins. The combination of the two coins is the offspring's genotype. Flip both coins together four times, and record the genotypes of the offspring.

_____

_____

_____

_____

9 Now flip your coins 100 times. Record the results on a separate piece of paper.

S.T.E.M. Lab continued

10 Use the result from your Punnett square analysis and coin tosses to complete the table.

RESULTS FROM PUNNETT SQUARE ANALYSIS AND COIN TOSSES

	Genotype			Phenotype	
	WW	*Ww*	*ww*	Widow's peak	Straight hairline
% predicted					
Actual % based on 4 coin tosses					
Actual % based on 100 coin tosses					

11 To observe the degree of scatter in the data, combine your results with that of other class members. A central place will be provided by your teacher where you can post your results and obtain results from others. Record the following class data in a second table.

COMBINED CLASS RESULTS FROM COIN TOSSES

	Student pair	% offspring with widow's peak phenotype
Actual % based on 4 coin tosses	1	
	2	
	3	
	4	
	5	
	6	
Actual % based on 100 coin tosses	1	
	2	
	3	
	4	
	5	
	6	

ANALYZE THE RESULTS

12 **Constructing Graphs** Make a bar graph to show the class results. Plot % offspring with widow's peak phenotype on the *y*-axis and student pair number on the *x*-axis.

S.T.E.M. Lab continued

13 **Describing Results** Based on your graph, which group of data show more scatter—the data from the smaller number of coin tosses or the data from the larger number of coin tosses? Explain.

_____

_____

_____

DRAW CONCLUSIONS

14 **Comparing Results** Do your results allow you to answer the question posed in Step 5? Explain.

_____

_____

_____

Connect TO THE ESSENTIAL QUESTION

15 **Applying Concepts** What have you learned in this lab about using large sample sizes? Why is it important that genetic studies be designed so that they test large sample sizes?

_____

_____

_____

_____

S.T.E.M. LAB GUIDED *Inquiry*

Matching Punnett Square Predictions

Punnett squares are used to predict the possible outcomes from the genetic cross of two parents. However, Punnett square analysis assumes that a sizeable number of offspring are produced. In this lab, you will observe the actual distribution of offspring phenotypes from some crosses and also determine the number of offspring necessary to accurately match a Punnett square prediction.

   You will follow a human trait during this analysis. The trait involves the shape of the hairline across the top of a person's forehead. If a person has a dominant allele (*W*) for this trait, their hairline forms a distinct point in the middle of the forehead called a widow's peak. People with straight hairlines have two recessive alleles (*w*) for this trait.

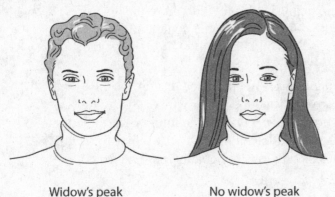

Widow's peak   No widow's peak

OBJECTIVES

• Use a Punnett square to predict the possible outcomes of a genetic cross.

• Compare the results of a simulated genetic cross to the outcomes predicted by a Punnett square.

MATERIALS

For each student pair
• marker
• paper, blank
• paper, graphing
• pennies (2)
• tape, masking
For each student
• safety goggles

PROCEDURE

RESEARCH A PROBLEM

❶ On a separate piece of paper, make a Punnett square for two parents who are both heterozygous (*Ww*) for the widow's peak trait.

❷ Complete the Punnett square for the offspring.

❸ Based on the Punnett square, what percentage of offspring will have the genotypes *WW, Ww,* and *ww*?

_____

_____

_____

S.T.E.M. Lab continued

4 Based on the Punnett square analysis, what are the expected phenotypes of these offspring? What percentage of the offspring is predicted to have a widow's peak? What percentage of the offspring is predicted to have a straight hairline?

_____

_____

_____

_____

ASK A QUESTION

5 A Punnett square analysis can be used to predict the outcomes of a genetic cross. However, does every actual cross always result in the outcome predicted by the Punnett square analysis? You will explore the answer to this question by carrying out your own simulated genetic crosses.

MAKE A PLAN

6 Decide on a procedure for doing a series of simulated test crosses. Be sure to have a way to represent the mother and the father with each having two alleles, W and w. Your plan should have a way to randomly determine the allele donated by the mother and the allele donated by the father for each offspring produced. Write your plan below and obtain your teacher's approval before beginning.

_____

_____

_____

_____

_____

MAKE OBSERVATIONS

7 Carry out four simulated crosses to produce four offspring. Record the genotypes of the offspring.

_____

_____

_____

_____

S.T.E.M. Lab continued

8 Now carry out 100 simulated crosses to produce 100 offspring. Record the results on a separate piece of paper.

9 Use the result from your Punnett square analysis and coin tosses to complete the table.

RESULTS FROM PUNNETT SQUARE ANALYSIS AND COIN TOSSES

	Genotype			Phenotype	
	WW	*Ww*	*ww*	Widow's peak	Straight hairline
% predicted					
Actual % based on 4 coin tosses					
Actual % based on 100 coin tosses					

10 To observe the degree of scatter in the data, combine your results with that of other class members. A central place will be provided by your teacher where you can post your results and obtain results from others. Record the following class data in a second table.

COMBINED CLASS RESULTS FROM COIN TOSSES

	Student pair	% offspring with widow's peak phenotype
Actual % based on 4 coin tosses	1	
	2	
	3	
	4	
	5	
	6	
Actual % based on 100 coin tosses	1	
	2	
	3	
	4	
	5	
	6	

S.T.E.M. Lab continued

ANALYZE THE RESULTS

⑪ **Constructing Graphs** Make a bar graph to show the class results. Plot % offspring with widow's peak phenotype on the *y*-axis and student pair number on the *x*-axis.

⑫ **Describing Results** Based on your graph, which group of data show more scatter—the data from the smaller number of coin tosses or the data from the larger number of coin tosses? Explain.

_____

_____

_____

DRAW CONCLUSIONS

⑬ **Comparing Results** Do your results allow you to answer the question posed in Step 5? Explain.

_____

_____

_____

Connect TO THE ESSENTIAL QUESTION

⑭ **Applying Concepts** What have you learned in this lab about using large sample sizes? Why is it important that genetic studies be designed so that they test large sample sizes?

_____

_____

_____

_____

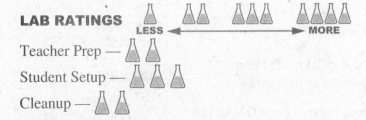

Modeling DNA GENERAL

👥 Student pairs

🕐 15 minutes

LAB RATINGS

LESS ←————————→ MORE

Teacher Prep —

Student Setup —

Cleanup —

| MATERIALS |
| For each pair |
| • craft beads, 2 colors (8 each) |
| • paper, blank |
| • paper clips, 4 colors (2 each) |
| • pipe cleaners (2) |
| For each student |
| • safety goggles |

SAFETY INFORMATION

Remind students to review all safety cautions and icons before beginning this lab. Students should handle pipe cleaners with caution to avoid injury. Spilled beads pose a falling hazard. Students should report and clean up spills immediately.

TEACHER NOTES

In this activity, students will construct a model of DNA and become acquainted with the pertinent terminology. Strips of colored construction paper may be substituted for the paper clips. To help students discover their own solutions to any problems, answer students' questions with other questions.

Tip This lab may help students understand how the structure of genetic material allows for the transfer of information across generations.

Skills Focus Making Models, Applying Concepts

| My Notes |
| _____ |
| _____ |
| _____ |
| _____ |
| _____ |

MODIFICATION FOR INDEPENDENT *Inquiry*

Challenge students to design models of DNA. Allow them to include whatever materials they like in their designs. Once you have approved their designs, allow them to build their models. Encourage students to examine their classmates' models, or have students present their models to the class.

Answer Key

3. Answers will vary.

6. Adenine is always paired with thymine, and guanine is always paired with cytosine.

7. nitrogenous base, nucleotide, gene, chromosome, nucleus, and cell

8. Sample answer: The paper clips, which represent nitrogenous bases, are the part that serves as a code. The unique combinations of nitrogenous bases are translated into proteins. This information is preserved in DNA and is passed on in the genes of offspring.

QUICK LAB DIRECTED *inquiry*

Modeling DNA

In this lab, you will construct a DNA model to illustrate the structure of genetic material.

PROCEDURE

1 Obtain 2 **pipe cleaners**, 8 each of 2 colors of **craft beads**, and 2 each of 4 colors of **paper clips** from your teacher.

2 Let the pipe cleaners represent the backbone of your DNA. The beads represent sugars and phosphates. The paper clips represent nitrogenous bases.

3 On a separate piece of **paper**, use colored pencils to make a color-coded key for your model. Be sure to name the nitrogenous bases for each color.

4 Use what you know about DNA to construct a model of one single strand of DNA. Include one of each of the four nitrogenous bases on this strand.

5 Use the remaining pipe cleaner, beads, and paperclips to make the complementary strand of DNA.

6 Which nitrogenous bases pair with each other?

_____

_____

_____

_____

7 To demonstrate the relationship of genetic material in the cell, put the following in order from smallest to largest: nucleus, chromosome, nucleotide, cell, nitrogenous base, and gene.

_____

_____

_____

_____

OBJECTIVES

- Construct a model of DNA.
- Describe the structure of DNA.

MATERIALS

For each pair
- craft beads, 2 colors (8 each)
- paper, blank
- paper clips, 4 colors (2 each)
- pipe cleaners (2)

For each student
- safety goggles

Quick Lab continued

8 DNA is often referred to as "the genetic code." What part of your model is the "code" that allows information to be stored in a cell and passed on to future generations? Explain your answer.

_____

_____

_____

_____

_____

_____

_____

_____

_____

_____

_____

QUICK LAB DIRECTED *Inquiry*

Building a DNA Sequence GENERAL

👤 Individual student

🕐 15 minutes

MATERIALS

For each student

- clay, modeling, 4 colors
- gloves
- lab apron

LAB RATINGS

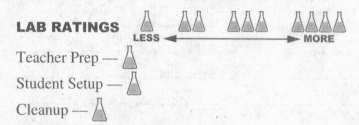

LESS ⟵————————⟶ MORE

Teacher Prep —

Student Setup —

Cleanup —

SAFETY INFORMATION

Remind students to review all safety cautions and icons before beginning this lab. Modeling clay can stain skin and clothing. Students should wear gloves and aprons while handling clay.

My Notes

_____

_____

_____

_____

_____

TEACHER NOTES

In this activity, students will use clay to model base pairing in a DNA strand. Students will need enough clay to make 12 small balls of each color. Point out to students that many biological molecules are built from smaller units called monomers. This activity may help students understand how biological polymers are built; however, it will not help them understand the shape of the DNA molecule. You may want to point out that DNA forms a double helix because of the way real nucleotides connect together.

Skills Focus Making Models, Applying Concepts

MODIFICATION FOR GUIDED *Inquiry*

Provide students with the modeling clay, and ask them to build a model of a small segment of DNA. You may also need to provide students with the list of base pairs and how they bond. Have students write a summary of what is shown in their model and what characteristics of DNA their model does not accurately represent.

Answer Key

2. Sample answer:

Nucleotide Base	Color	Nucleotide Base	Color
A	red	G	green
T	blue	C	yellow

3. Sample answer: TTAGACCAGTGCAAGTTCAGCCGT

4. Sample answer: AATCTGGTCACGTTCAAGTCGGCA

   Teacher Prompt Which base matches with adenine (A)? Which one matches with guanine (G)? Sample answer: Thymine (T) bonds with adenine. Cytosine (C) bonds with guanine.

5. Sample answer: They did not use the same color clay that I used for each type of nucleotide. They connected the nucleotides to form a different sequence than I made. We all had the same base pairings.

6. Sample answer: The strand codes for eight amino acids. It contains 24 bases, and each group of three bases codes for one amino acid. 24/3 = 8.

Building a DNA Sequence

Many molecules in the body, such as DNA, RNA, and proteins, are built by joining smaller molecules together to make large molecules. In this activity, you will make a model of a DNA molecule. You will use clay balls to model the building blocks of DNA, which are called nucleotides.

A nucleotide contains one of four molecules called bases. There are four types of DNA bases—adenine (A), guanine (G), cytosine (C), and thymine (T). In DNA, the bases bond together in a specific way. Adenine binds only with thymine, and guanine binds only with cytosine.

OBJECTIVES

- Describe how DNA is made up of smaller molecules.
- Make a model DNA sequence.

MATERIALS

For each student
- clay, modeling, 4 colors
- gloves
- lab apron

PROCEDURE

❶ Make 12 equal-sized **clay balls** of each color.

❷ Choose which color will represent each nucleotide. Record your choices in the table below.

Nucleotide Base	Color	Nucleotide Base	Color
A		G	
T		C	

❸ Connect 24 balls (six of each color) together in any order. Record the order of the bases below.

_____

❹ Make a DNA strand that is complementary to the one you made in Step 3 by matching each base in your original strand with the base it bonds to. For example, every T in your original strand should be matched to an A in your new strand. Record the order of the bases in your new strand below.

_____

Quick Lab continued

5 Compare and contrast your piece of DNA with other students' pieces.

_____

_____

_____

_____

_____

6 In DNA, a group of three nucleotides is a code for one of the 20 amino acids used to make proteins. Chemicals in cells "read" the nucleotides in DNA and translate them into proteins. How many amino acids does your DNA strand code for? Explain your answer.

_____

_____

_____

_____

_____

QUICK LAB DIRECTED Inquiry

Mutations Cause Diversity GENERAL

Individual student

15 minutes

LAB RATINGS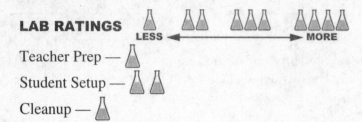

LESS ◄————————► MORE

Teacher Prep —

Student Setup —

Cleanup —

MATERIALS

For the class
• stopwatch

For each student
• beads, blue, green, orange, and yellow
• safety goggles
• sewing needle
• string, 20 cm in length

SAFETY INFORMATION

Remind students to review all safety cautions and icons before beginning this lab. Spilled beads are a slipping hazard. Students should clean up all spills immediately. Caution students to handle sewing needles carefully in order to avoid puncture wounds.

TEACHER NOTES

In this activity, students explore how mutations happen when using RNA code to make protein chains. In order for students to have mutations appear in their string of beads, they should feel comfortable with the possibility of having an incorrect order of beads.

   If all students are able to complete their chains correctly within the allotted 30 seconds, try giving them a new code and reduce the allotted time until students start making mistakes. The point of the exercise is to illustrate that errors arise within a population. If desired, beads and pipe cleaners can be used in place of sewing needles and string.

Tip This exercise may help students understand how errors in protein translation lead to diversity.

Student Tip If you make a mistake, just keep stringing beads.

Skills Focus Making Models, Applying Concepts, Comparing Results

My Notes

_____

_____

_____

_____

_____

MODIFICATION FOR GUIDED Inquiry

Ask students how they can use the materials provided to model the production of protein from a strand of RNA. Once they have come up with a code and a method of assembly, ask them to make their code and string of beads increasingly longer. Encourage them to assemble their strands as quickly as possible. Ask students how the length of their strands and the speed of assembly affected their accuracy. Lead a discussion of how such errors actually occur in real protein synthesis, and ask students how such errors would affect the diversity of a population.

Answer Key

5. CCU | CUU | CCU | GUC | CUA | UCC | CUU

    red   blue   red orange blue yellow blue

6. Answers will vary.

7. Answers will vary.

8. Answers will vary.

QUICK LAB DIRECTED *Inquiry*

Mutations Cause Diversity

In this lab, you will simulate the process of making proteins from RNA code in order to demonstrate how errors in translation lead to diversity.

PROCEDURE

1 Thread a piece of **string** on a **needle.** Tie a knot in the string at the end opposite the needle.

2 Your teacher has provided you with **beads** of various colors. These beads represent amino acids. You will use an RNA code to determine the order in which you must place the amino acid beads on your string.

3 When your teacher tells you to begin, use the RNA code and the chart below to place the beads on your string in the correct order. You will have 30 seconds to string your beads.

OBJECTIVE

• Explain how protein translation errors cause mutations.

MATERIALS

For the class
• stopwatch

For each student
• beads, blue, green, orange, and yellow
• safety goggles
• sewing needle
• string, 20 cm in length

Code:

C C U C U U C C U G U C C U A U C C C U U

Key:

Code	CUU	CCU	UUC	UCC	GUC	CUA
Color	blue	red	green	yellow	orange	blue

4 After you've completed your string of beads, tie a knot at the top.

5 Write the full code in the space below. Draw lines after every three letters in the code. Under each triplet of letters, write the correct color of bead.

Quick Lab continued

6 Check your string of beads. Are any of the colors wrong?

_____

_____

_____

7 If yes, figure out what caused the mistake. Is it like any of the types of mutation you have studied in class?

_____

_____

_____

_____

_____

_____

_____

8 Compare your string of beads with those of your classmates. Do they all look the same? How do the results of the entire class relate to genetic diversity?

_____

_____

_____

_____

_____

_____

EXPLORATION LAB DIRECTED Inquiry **OR** GUIDED Inquiry

Extracting DNA GENERAL

👥 Student pairs

🕐 45 minutes

LAB RATINGS

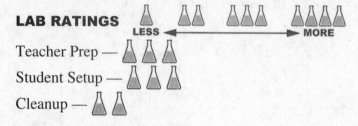

LESS ←————→ MORE

Teacher Prep —

Student Setup —

Cleanup —

SAFETY INFORMATION

Remind students to review all safety cautions and icons before beginning this lab. Students should wear goggles, gloves, and aprons at all times during this activity. Wipe up all spills immediately. Check for any student allergies to raw wheat germ.

TEACHER NOTES

In this activity, students will use common household items to release, unravel, and collect DNA. They will extract DNA from raw wheat germ, which is part of the seed of a wheat plant. Make sure to use raw (not toasted) wheat germ; toasted wheat germ will not yield any DNA. Chill the isopropyl alcohol before class by setting it in an ice bath. The hot water students use should be approximately 55 °C.

Tip This activity may help students better understand that DNA is composed of long, coiled strands.

Skills Focus Practicing Lab Techniques, Making Observations

MODIFICATION FOR INDEPENDENT Inquiry

A strand of DNA is shaped like a twisted ladder, with two "rails" running parallel to each other and "rungs" in between. The twisted shape is called a double helix. Have students research and then build a model of a DNA double helix. They should create a procedure for building their model, including where they will research its shape and the materials they will use to build it. With teacher approval, they should build their models and then present them to the class.

MATERIALS

For each pair
- glass rod, 8 cm long
- glass slide
- inoculating loop
- isopropyl alcohol, cold (15 mL)
- soap, liquid dishwashing (1 mL)
- table salt
- test tube or beaker, 50 mL
- water, hot tap (20 mL)
- wheat germ, raw (1 g)

For each student
- gloves
- lab apron
- safety goggles

My Notes

_____

_____

_____

_____

_____

Exploration Lab continued

Answer Key for DIRECTED Inquiry

FORM A HYPOTHESIS

2. Sample answer: I think the DNA will be very long because DNA molecules are long strands.

ANALYZE THE RESULTS

10. Answers may vary. Students should describe the color as clear or white, and a viscosity that is similar to mucus. The length of the DNA sample may differ; it may be several short strands or a single giant thread. Some students may note its sticky texture and elastic nature.

11. Sample answer: Detergent breaks down and emulsifies the fat and proteins that make up the cell membrane and the nuclear membrane, causing the DNA to be released into solution. Heat softens the cell and nuclear membranes and inactivates (denatures) some enzymes that cut DNA into small fragments. Alcohol causes the DNA to precipitate out of solution. This allows the DNA to be collected and helps to partially purify the DNA from other cellular components that are soluble in water but not alcohol.

DRAW CONCLUSIONS

12. Answers will vary but should include how the characteristics of the alcohol, detergent, and water temperatures are related to their proposed roles in DNA extraction.

Connect TO THE ESSENTIAL QUESTION

13. Sample answer: The sample sticks to itself, which relates to the double helix structure. It also forms long strings, which relates to the fact that eukaryotic DNA is very long.

Answer Key for GUIDED Inquiry

FORM A HYPOTHESIS

2. Sample answer: I think the DNA will be very long because DNA molecules are long strands.

ANALYZE THE RESULTS

10. Answers may vary. Students should describe the color as clear or white, and a viscosity that is similar to mucus. The length of the DNA sample may differ; it may be several short strands or a single giant thread. Some students may note its sticky texture and elastic nature.

11. Sample answer: Detergent breaks down and emulsifies the fat and proteins that make up the cell membrane and the nuclear membrane, causing the DNA to be released into solution. Heat softens the cell and nuclear membranes and inactivates (denatures) some enzymes that cut DNA into small fragments. Alcohol causes the DNA to precipitate out of solution. This allows the DNA to be collected and helps to partially purify the DNA from other cellular components that are soluble in water but not alcohol.

DRAW CONCLUSIONS

12. Answers will vary but should include how the characteristics of the alcohol, detergent, and water temperatures are related to their proposed roles in DNA extraction. Hypotheses should include both a prediction and an explanation for that prediction. The proposed experimental procedures should relate directly to the hypothesis.

Connect TO THE ESSENTIAL QUESTION

13. Sample answer: The sample sticks to itself, which relates to the double helix structure. It also forms long strings, which relates to the fact that eukaryotic DNA is very long. The DNA in prokaryotic cells is shorter.

EXPLORATION LAB `DIRECTED` *Inquiry*

Extracting DNA

In this lab, you will extract and study the DNA from raw wheat germ.

PROCEDURE

ASK A QUESTION

① In this lab, you will investigate the following question:
How can you extract the DNA from plant material?

FORM A HYPOTHESIS

② In this lab, you will extract the DNA from raw wheat germ.
What do you think the DNA will look like to your unaided eye?
Explain your answer.

_____

_____

_____

_____

TEST THE HYPOTHESIS

③ Place 1 g of **wheat germ** into a clean **test tube**.

④ Add 20 mL **hot tap water** and stir with a **glass rod** for 2 to 3
minutes.

⑤ Add a pinch of **table salt** to the material in the test tube and mix
it well.

⑥ Add a few drops (1 mL) of **liquid dishwashing soap** to the
liquid in the test tube. Stir the mixture with the glass rod for 1 minute until it
is well mixed.

OBJECTIVES

- Extract DNA from
  wheat germ.
- Observe the
  structure of DNA.

MATERIALS

For each student pair
- glass rod, 8 cm long
- glass slide
- inoculating loop
- isopropyl alcohol,
  cold (15 mL)
- soap, liquid
  dishwashing (1 mL)
- table salt
- test tube or beaker,
  50 mL
- water, hot tap
  (20 mL)
- wheat germ, raw
  (1 g)

For each student
- gloves
- lab apron
- safety goggles

Exploration Lab continued

7 Tilt the test tube slightly. Slowly pour 15 mL **cold isopropyl alcohol** down the side of the tilted tube. The alcohol should form a top layer over the original solution. Note: Do not pour the alcohol too fast or directly into the wheat germ solution.

8 Tilt the tube upright. After about 10–15 minutes, a stringy, white material should float up into the alcohol layer. This material is the DNA from the wheat germ.

9 Carefully insert the **inoculating loop** into the white material in the alcohol layer. Gently twist the loop as you wind the DNA around the loop. Remove the loop from the tube, and tap the DNA onto a **glass slide**.

ANALYZE THE RESULTS

10 **Describing Events** Describe the appearance of the DNA on the slide.

_____

_____

_____

_____

11 **Interpreting Information** Explain the role of detergent, heat, and isopropyl alcohol in the extraction of DNA.

_____

_____

_____

_____

DRAW CONCLUSIONS

12 **Designing Methods** Design a DNA extraction experiment in which you explore the effect of changing the variables.

_____

_____

_____

_____

_____

_____

_____

Exploration Lab continued

Connect TO THE ESSENTIAL QUESTION

⑬ **Comparing Information** How do the characteristics of your DNA sample relate to the structure of eukaryotic DNA?

_____

_____

_____

_____

_____

EXPLORATION LAB GUIDED Inquiry

Extracting DNA

In this lab, you will extract and study the DNA from raw wheat germ.

PROCEDURE

ASK A QUESTION

1 In this lab, you will investigate the following question: How can you extract the DNA from plant material?

FORM A HYPOTHESIS

2 In this lab, you will extract the DNA from raw wheat germ. What do you think the DNA will look like to your unaided eye? Explain your answer.

_____

_____

_____

_____

_____

TEST THE HYPOTHESIS

3 Place 1 g of **wheat germ** into a clean **test tube**.

4 Add 20 mL **hot tap water** and stir with a **glass rod** for 2 to 3 minutes.

5 Add a pinch of **table salt** to the material in the test tube and mix it well.

6 Add a few drops (1 mL) of **liquid dishwashing soap** to the liquid in the test tube. Stir the mixture with the glass rod for 1 minute until it is well mixed.

> ## OBJECTIVES
>
> - Extract DNA from wheat germ.
> - Observe the structure of DNA.
>
> ## MATERIALS
>
> For each student pair
> - glass rod, 8 cm long
> - glass slide
> - inoculating loop
> - isopropyl alcohol, cold (15 mL)
> - soap, liquid dishwashing (1 mL)
> - table salt
> - test tube or beaker, 50 mL
> - water, hot tap (20 mL)
> - wheat germ, raw (1 g)
>
> For each student
> - gloves
> - lab apron
> - safety goggles

Exploration Lab continued

7 Tilt the test tube slightly. Slowly pour 15 mL **cold isopropyl alcohol** down the side of the tilted tube. The alcohol should form a top layer over the original solution. Note: Do not pour the alcohol too fast or directly into the wheat germ solution.

8 Tilt the tube upright. After about 10–15 minutes, a stringy, white material should float up into the alcohol layer. This material is the DNA from the wheat germ.

9 Carefully insert the **inoculating loop** into the white material in the alcohol layer. Gently twist the loop as you wind the DNA around the loop. Remove the loop from the tube, and tap the DNA onto a **glass slide**.

ANALYZE THE RESULTS

10 **Describing Events** Describe the appearance of the DNA on the slide in detail. Draw a labeled diagram of what you see.

_____

_____

_____

_____

_____

Exploration Lab continued

11 **Interpreting Information** Explain the role of detergent, heat, and isopropyl alcohol in the extraction of DNA.

_____

_____

_____

_____

DRAW CONCLUSIONS

12 **Designing Methods** Design a DNA extraction experiment in which you explore the effect of changing the variables. Write a hypothesis for your experiment, and explain how your procedure will help you test your hypothesis.

_____

_____

_____

_____

_____

_____

_____

_____

_____

_____

_____

_____

_____

_____

_____

_____

_____

Connect TO THE ESSENTIAL QUESTION

13 **Comparing Information** How do the characteristics of your DNA sample relate to the structure of eukaryotic DNA? Compare the characteristics you witness to those of prokaryotic cells.

_____

_____

_____

_____

_____

_____

_____

_____

_____

_____

_____

_____

_____

_____

QUICK LAB GUIDED *Inquiry*

How Can a Simple Code Be Used to Make a Product? GENERAL

👥 Individual student

🕙 30 minutes

LAB RATINGS

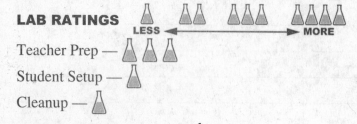

LESS ◄————————► MORE

Teacher Prep —

Student Setup —

Cleanup —

MATERIALS

For each student
- bottle, clear plastic
- code sheet
- colored pencils
- cups, paper (4)
- funnel
- lab apron
- safety goggles
- sand, colored (4 colors)
- spoon

SAFETY INFORMATION

Remind students to review all safety cautions and icons before beginning this lab.

TEACHER NOTES

In this activity, students will decipher a numeric code in order to make sand sculptures with the colors in the correct order. Before class begins, make code sheets using numbers for letters where 1 = A and 26 = Z. As an example, 18-5-4 would equal RED. Each code should specify 8 to 12 colored layers. Give each group a different code in order to produce a variety of patterns.

Skills Focus Solving Problems, Comparing Results, Applying Concepts

My Notes

_____

_____

_____

_____

_____

MODIFICATION FOR DIRECTED *Inquiry*

To make decoding easier, you may give students the key to deciphering their code.

MODIFICATION FOR INDEPENDENT *Inquiry*

Ask students to create their own codes. Have partners exchange and decipher one another's codes.

Answer Key

1. Answers will vary.

9. No

10. Sample answer. The colors of their sand are in a different order in their sculptures.

11. No. The sculpture would be the same if they had the same secret code as our group.

12. Sample answer. The code told us the order of colors in our sculpture.

Quick Lab continued

13. Answers will vary. Examples are UPC codes, Braille, Morse code.

14. DNA

15. Sample answer: You would look for parent organisms that exhibited the traits that you desire because those organisms would contain the genetic code for those desirable traits.

QUICK LAB GUIDED *Inquiry*

How Can a Simple Code Be Used to Make a Product?

In this lab, you will make a layered sand sculpture. You will decipher a secret code to put the layers of the sculpture in the right order.

PROCEDURE

1 Obtain a **secret code** from your teacher.

2 Decipher your code to find the order and colors of sand to use in your sculpture.

3 What steps did you take to decipher your secret code?

_____

_____

4 Obtain a **clear plastic bottle**, a **spoon**, and a **funnel** from your teacher.

5 Obtain **paper cups full of colored sand** that you will use to make your sand sculpture.

6 Use your funnel to place 4 spoonfuls of the first color of sand specified in your code into the bottle.

7 Repeat Step 6 for the other colors of sand in your code, making sure to follow the order in your deciphered code. Sketch your sculpture below. Use **colored pencils** to shade the sand in your drawing.

OBJECTIVES
- Decipher a numeric code.
- Describe how DNA codes for protein.

MATERIALS

For each student
- bottle, clear plastic
- code sheet
- colored pencils
- cups, paper (4)
- funnel
- lab apron
- safety goggles
- sand, colored (4 colors)
- spoon

Quick Lab continued

8 Look at the sculptures made by other groups in your class.

9 Are their sculptures the same as yours or different?

_____

10 If different, how are they different?

_____

_____

11 Do you think they had the same secret code as your group? Why or why not?

_____

_____

12 How did your secret code help you to create your sand sculpture?

_____

_____

13 How are codes sometimes used in everyday life?

_____

_____

_____

_____

14 What is considered to be the code of life?

_____

_____

15 If you wanted to produce an organism, such as a cow that produced a lot of milk or corn that tasted sweet, what would you look for in the parent organisms?

_____

_____

_____

_____

QUICK LAB DIRECTED Inquiry

Observing Selective Breeding GENERAL

👤 Individual student

🕐 20 minutes

LAB RATINGS

LESS ←——————→ MORE

Teacher Prep —

Student Setup —

Cleanup —

MATERIALS

For each student
- colored pencils
- reference materials

My Notes

_____

_____

_____

_____

_____

TEACHER NOTES

In this activity, students will study a diagram of *Brassica oleracea,* or wild cabbage, and analyze how selective breeding was used to produce new species of vegetables. Students will draw pictures of the new species of vegetables and compare them to the diagram provided of *B. oleracea.* You may want to provide pictures of each type of vegetable for students who do not know what they are.

Skills Focus Making Comparisons, Drawing Conclusions

MODIFICATION FOR GUIDED Inquiry

Tell students that broccoli, brussels sprouts, cauliflower, kale, and kohlrabi were all bred from *Brassica oleracea* using selective breeding. Have each student come up with a procedure to determine which characteristics of *B. oleracea* were selected for each new vegetable. Review students' procedures to approve them. If reasonable, allow students to carry out their procedures.

MODIFICATION FOR INDEPENDENT Inquiry

Tell students that some of the vegetables found in the produce section of the supermarket have been selectively bred from the wild cabbage, *Brassica oleracea.* Have each student hypothesize which vegetables they are and write a procedure to test the hypothesis. Allow students to carry out any reasonable procedures.

Quick Lab continued

Answer Key

3.

Vegetable	Drawing	Similarities
Broccoli	Student drawings should resemble broccoli.	similar flowering stems
Brussels sprouts	Student drawings should resemble brussels sprouts.	similar buds
Cauliflower	Student drawings should resemble cauliflower.	similar flowering stems
Kale	Student drawings should resemble kale.	similar loose leaves
Kohlrabi	Student drawings should resemble kohlrabi.	similar stems

4. Accept any reasonable response.

5. Accept any reasonable response.

6. Leaves, buds, stems, and flowering structures.

QUICK LAB DIRECTED *Inquiry*

Observing Selective Breeding

In this lab, you will study how selective breeding is used to produce new vegetables. *Brassica oleracea*, or wild cabbage, has been cultivated and eaten for at least 2,500 years. By using selective breeding, different vegetables have been cultivated from it, including broccoli, brussels sprouts, cauliflower, kale, and kohlrabi.

PROCEDURE

1 Study the diagram of the *Brassica oleracea*.

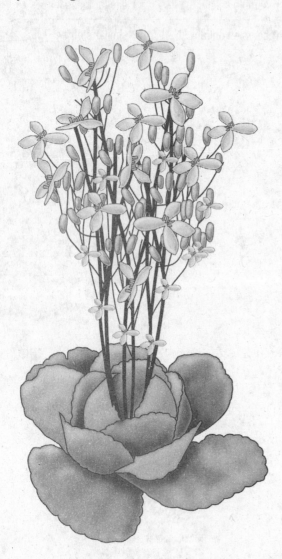

OBJECTIVE

• Describe how new species of plants have been produced through selective breeding.

MATERIALS

For each student

• colored pencils

• reference materials

Quick Lab continued

2 In the chart below, use **colored pencils** to draw pictures of each vegetable. Use **reference materials** if needed.

Vegetable	Drawing	Similarities to *B. oleracea*
Broccoli		
Brussels sprouts		
Cauliflower		
Kale		
Kohlrabi		

3 Compare your drawings to the diagram of the *brassica oleracea*. Write in the chart how the modern vegetables are similar to the *B. oleracea*.

4 Which new vegetable do you think most closely resembles the *B. oleracea*? Explain your choice.

_____

_____

_____

_____

5 Which new vegetable do you think least resembles the *B. oleracea*? Explain your choice.

_____

_____

_____

_____

Quick Lab continued

6 Which characteristics of the *B. oleracea* have been selected to produce new vegetables?

_____

_____

_____

_____

_____

_____

_____

_____